SHANGHAI
Travel Guide 2024

The Updated Guide to an Unforgettable Journey to the City of Dreams

Michael G. Simmons

2024 Edition

Copyright © 2024 by Michael G. Simmons

All rights reserved. No part of this publication may be reproduced, distributed, or transmitted in any form or by any means, including photocopying, recording, or other electronic or mechanical methods, without the prior written permission of the publisher, except in the case of brief quotations embodied in critical reviews and certain other noncommercial uses permitted by copyright law.

Disclaimer

The information contained in this guide is for general informational purposes only. While every effort has been made to provide accurate and up-to-date information, the author makes no representations or warranties of any kind, express or implied, about the completeness, accuracy, reliability, suitability, or availability with respect to the content provided. Any reliance you place on such information is, therefore, strictly at your own risk.

In no event will the author be liable for any loss or damage, including without limitation, indirect or consequential loss or damage, or any loss or damage whatsoever arising from the information contained within. The inclusion of any links does not necessarily imply a recommendation or endorse the views expressed within them. This guide is meant for informational purposes and should be cross-verified with updated official resources before making travel-related decisions.

Table of Contents

Introduction to Shanghai.. 6

    A Brief Overview of Shanghai, Including its History, Culture, and Economy............................. 7

    Reasons to Visit Shanghai...................................... 10

    When to Visit Shanghai... 13

Chapter 1: Planning Your Trip to Shanghai.......... 18

    Visa and Passport Requirements........................... 18

    Currency Exchange... 21

    Transportation to and from Shanghai.................... 23

    Accommodation Options in Shanghai................... 27

    Booking Tips & Websites.. 36

    What to Pack for a Trip to Shanghai..................... 38

Chapter 2: Exploring Shanghai's Neighborhoods. 42

    The Bund... 42

    The French Concession.. 45

    Xintiandi.. 48

    Jing'an... 51

Pudong...53

Chapter 3: Must-See Attractions in Shanghai........ 58

The Oriental Pearl Tower....................................... 58

The Shanghai Museum... 61

The Yu Garden... 64

The Jade Buddha Temple..................................... 66

The Bund Sightseeing Tunnel............................... 69

Chapter 4: Shanghai's Culinary Scene................... 72

Traditional Shanghainese Cuisine......................... 72

Street Food in Shanghai....................................... 76

Upscale Dining in Shanghai.................................. 79

Nightlife in Shanghai... 82

Chapter 5: Shopping in Shanghai........................... 86

The Best Places to Shop in Shanghai................... 86

What to Buy in Shanghai....................................... 88

Bargaining Tips for Shopping in Shanghai............ 91

Chapter 6: Cultural Experiences in Shanghai....... 96

Attending a Traditional Chinese Opera

Performance..96

Visiting a Teahouse................................. 98

Taking a Calligraphy Class.................................101

Learning to Make Dumplings..............................103

Going on a Walking Tour of the City................. 105

Chapter 7: Day Trips from Shanghai....................110

Suzhou: A city of Canals and Gardens................110

Hangzhou: A Picturesque City on West Lake..... 112

Nanjing: The Former Capital of Six Dynasties... 114

How to Get There... 116

Chapter 8: Practical Information for Visitors..... 120

Language and Communication..........................120

Etiquette and Customs...122

Health and Safety Tips.. 125

Emergency Contact Information......................... 128

Chapter 9: Travel Cost... 130

Average Daily Expenses for Budget, Mid-range, and Luxury travelers..130

Factors that Can Affect Your Travel Costs..........133

Chapter 10: Further Exploration..........................138

Additional Resources for Planning Your Trip to Shanghai... 138

Suggested Itineraries for Different Types of Travelers... 141

Tips for Planning Your Itinerary..........................144

Conclusion.. 148

Introduction to Shanghai

Imagine a city where the past and future collide, where ancient traditions intertwine with cutting-edge innovation, where bustling streets teem with energy and tranquility coexists in serene gardens. This is Shanghai, a city that has captured the hearts of travelers for centuries and continues to mesmerize with its ever-evolving charm.

From its humble beginnings as a fishing village, Shanghai has risen to become a global metropolis, a testament to its resilience and the indomitable spirit of its people. Today, it stands as a beacon of modernity, a hub of commerce, and a cultural melting pot that embraces diversity with open arms.

But beneath the gleaming skyscrapers and vibrant neon lights, Shanghai's soul lies in its rich heritage and the warmth of its people. The narrow alleyways of the Old Town whisper tales of bygone eras, while the teahouses offer a glimpse into the city's time-honored traditions. In the bustling markets, the aroma of spices and the lively chatter of vendors create an intoxicating symphony of sights, sounds, and smells.

Shanghai is a city that awakens the senses, a place where every corner holds a new discovery, every encounter sparks an unforgettable memory. From the serene beauty of Yuyuan Gardens to the exhilarating heights of the Oriental Pearl Tower, Shanghai's tapestry of experiences is woven with endless possibilities.

Whether you're seeking culinary adventures, cultural immersion, or simply a chance to wander and soak in the city's vibrant atmosphere, Shanghai promises an unforgettable journey. Prepare to be captivated by its allure, to have your senses awakened, and to discover a city that truly captures the essence of modern China.

A Brief Overview of Shanghai, Including its History, Culture, and Economy

History
Shanghai, a city with a rich history dating back over 2,000 years, has undergone a remarkable transformation from a small fishing village to a global metropolis. Its strategic location on the Huangpu River, the gateway to the Yangtze River Delta, has played a pivotal role in its development.

During the Tang Dynasty (618-907 AD), Shanghai emerged as a significant port city, and its importance grew further during the Song Dynasty (960-1279 AD) due to its thriving maritime trade. In the 19th century, Shanghai became a major center of foreign trade and cultural exchange, and its international influence continued to grow in the 20th century.

Today, Shanghai stands as a testament to China's rapid economic development and is considered a symbol of the country's modernization. Its skyline is dominated by towering skyscrapers, and its streets are bustling with activity, reflecting the city's dynamic and cosmopolitan character.

Culture
Shanghai's culture is a vibrant blend of traditional Chinese customs and modern influences. The city is home to numerous historical landmarks, including the iconic Bund waterfront and the serene Yuyuan Gardens. Traditional Chinese arts, such as calligraphy, tea ceremonies, and opera performances, thrive alongside contemporary art galleries, trendy fashion boutiques, and cutting-edge restaurants.

The city's culinary scene is a culinary delight, offering a diverse array of flavors from various regions of

China. Street food stalls tempt passersby with their aromas, while upscale restaurants showcase the city's culinary prowess. Shanghai's nightlife is equally vibrant, with lively bars, clubs, and karaoke lounges catering to every taste.

Economy

Shanghai is the economic powerhouse of China, serving as a major hub for finance, trade, and manufacturing. The city is home to the world's busiest container port, the Port of Shanghai, and is a key player in China's global trade. Shanghai's financial sector is also highly developed, with the Shanghai Stock Exchange being one of the world's largest by market capitalization.

The city's economy is characterized by its rapid growth and innovation. Shanghai is a pioneer in various industries, including biotechnology, artificial intelligence, and e-commerce. Its entrepreneurial spirit and commitment to innovation have fueled its economic success and solidified its position as a global leader.

Reasons to Visit Shanghai

Shanghai, a city of captivating contrasts and boundless energy, beckons travelers with a myriad of reasons to explore its vibrant streets, immerse in its rich culture, and experience its unique blend of tradition and modernity. From culinary delights to cultural immersions, Shanghai promises an unforgettable journey that will awaken your senses and leave you yearning for more.

1. Culinary Adventures

Shanghai's culinary scene is a symphony of flavors, a testament to the city's diverse history and cultural influences. Embark on a gastronomic adventure and savor the authentic tastes of Shanghai, from delicate Shanghainese cuisine to hearty street food delights. Indulge in Xiao Long Bao, the city's signature soup dumplings, or tantalize your taste buds with the fiery flavors of Sichuan cuisine. From Michelin-starred restaurants to bustling street food stalls, Shanghai's culinary tapestry is woven with endless possibilities.

2. Cultural Immersion

Delve into the heart of Shanghai's rich culture, where ancient traditions intertwine with modern expressions. Wander through the enchanting Yuyuan Gardens, a

UNESCO World Heritage Site, and immerse yourself in the tranquility of traditional Chinese gardens. Witness the elegance of a traditional Chinese opera performance, or let the enchanting melodies of a guzheng serenade soothe your soul. Explore the city's art museums, brimming with masterpieces that span centuries, or discover the vibrant contemporary art scene that pulsates with creativity.

3. Architectural Marvels

Gaze upon the awe-inspiring skyline of Shanghai, where towering skyscrapers pierce the clouds, symbolizing the city's relentless pursuit of progress. Ascend the Oriental Pearl Tower, an iconic landmark, and marvel at the panoramic views of the city's sprawling expanse. Stroll along the Bund, the city's historic waterfront promenade, and admire the architectural grandeur of colonial-era buildings juxtaposed against modern skyscrapers.

4. Shopping Extravaganza

Indulge your shopping desires in Shanghai's bustling markets and luxurious boutiques. From the vibrant Nanjing Road, a shopper's paradise, to the trendy boutiques of Xintiandi, Shanghai caters to every taste and budget. Discover unique treasures in antique shops, haggle for bargains in bustling markets, and browse the latest designer fashions in upscale malls.

5. Nightlife Delights
Immerse yourself in Shanghai's vibrant nightlife, where neon lights illuminate the streets and a contagious energy fills the air. From rooftop bars with breathtaking city views to lively jazz clubs and pulsating nightclubs, Shanghai's nightlife scene offers an electrifying mix of entertainment. Dance the night away to the rhythm of electronic beats, savor cocktails in sophisticated lounges, or unwind with live music performances.

6. Day Trips and Excursions
Venture beyond Shanghai's bustling streets and explore the surrounding regions, each with its unique charm and historical significance. Discover the serene beauty of Suzhou, a city of canals and gardens, or immerse yourself in the picturesque landscapes of Hangzhou, renowned for its enchanting West Lake. Delve into the rich history of Nanjing, the former capital of six dynasties, and explore its ancient city walls and imperial tombs.

7. A City of Contrasts
Shanghai's allure lies in its captivating contrasts, where tradition and modernity coexist, where ancient temples stand amidst towering skyscrapers, and where bustling streets give way to tranquil gardens. Experience the city's vibrant energy as you navigate through its bustling markets, then find solace in the serenity of its temples. Witness the city's rapid transformation as you explore its historic neighborhoods, then marvel at its architectural marvels that symbolize its relentless pursuit of progress.

8. A City of Dreams
Shanghai is a city of dreams, where possibilities are endless and aspirations take flight. It is a place where the past and future collide, where ancient traditions intertwine with cutting-edge innovation, and where the spirit of entrepreneurship thrives. Embrace the city's infectious energy, let its vibrant culture captivate you, and discover the endless possibilities that await in Shanghai, a city that truly captures the essence of modern China.

When to Visit Shanghai

Shanghai, a city that embraces all seasons, offers a unique blend of experiences throughout the year. From the vibrant blooms of spring to the festive cheer of winter, each season presents its own distinct charms and attractions. Whether you seek the warmth of the sun or the crispness of the winter air, Shanghai has something to offer every traveler, making it a truly versatile destination.

Spring (March-May)
As the city awakens from its winter slumber, spring brings a burst of color and vibrancy to Shanghai. The parks and gardens come alive with blooming flowers, while the streets are filled with the joyous sounds of outdoor activities. Spring is an ideal time to explore Shanghai's outdoor attractions, such as the Yuyuan Gardens and the Bund, while enjoying the pleasant temperatures and comfortable weather.

Summer (June-August)
Shanghai's summers are characterized by warm temperatures, lively festivals, and a vibrant atmosphere. The city comes alive with energy as locals and tourists take to the streets to enjoy the summer festivities. The Dragon Boat Festival, celebrated in June, showcases colorful boat races and traditional performances. Summer is also a great time to explore Shanghai's beaches and enjoy the refreshing waters of the East China Sea.

Autumn (September-November)
Autumn brings a welcome respite from the summer heat, as the temperatures become milder and the air turns crisp. The city's parks and gardens are adorned with fiery autumn foliage, creating a picturesque backdrop for leisurely strolls. Autumn is also a popular time for festivals, such as the Mid-Autumn Festival, which celebrates the harvest moon with mooncakes, lanterns, and vibrant celebrations.

Winter (December-February)
Shanghai's winters are pleasantly cool, with occasional snowfall that transforms the city into a winter wonderland. The city takes on a festive atmosphere during the Christmas and New Year holidays, with twinkling lights and holiday decorations adorning the streets and buildings. Winter is an ideal time to indulge in the city's culinary delights, as warm soups, hot pots, and traditional Shanghainese cuisine provide a comforting escape from the chilly weather.

Considerations for Choosing Your Travel Dates

When planning your trip to Shanghai, consider the following factors:
Weather: Spring and autumn offer the most pleasant temperatures for exploring the city comfortably.

Summer can be hot and humid, while winter can be cool and occasionally snowy.

Crowds: Shanghai is a popular tourist destination year-round, but peak seasons, such as summer and national holidays, tend to be more crowded. If you prefer a more relaxed experience, consider visiting during the shoulder seasons of spring or autumn.

Festivals and Events: Shanghai hosts a variety of festivals and events throughout the year. If you're interested in experiencing a particular festival or event, plan your trip accordingly.

Ultimately, the best time to visit Shanghai depends on your personal preferences and what you hope to experience during your trip. With its diverse attractions and captivating atmosphere, Shanghai offers something to enjoy for every traveler, no matter the season.

Chapter 1: Planning Your Trip to Shanghai

Embark on a seamless journey to Shanghai with this comprehensive guide to visa requirements, currency exchange, transportation options, accommodation choices, and essential packing tips.

Visa and Passport Requirements

To ensure a seamless travel experience to Shanghai, it is crucial to understand the visa and passport requirements for your nationality. Whether you are a tourist seeking to explore the city's vibrant attractions or a business traveler attending a conference, knowing the necessary documentation will streamline your entry process.

Tourist Visas (L Visas)

If your primary purpose in Shanghai is to engage in leisure activities such as sightseeing, visiting friends and family, or attending cultural events, you will require a Tourist Visa (L Visa). This visa is valid for up to 60 days, providing ample time to immerse yourself in the city's captivating atmosphere.

Business Visas (F Visas)
For those embarking on business-related endeavors in Shanghai, such as attending conferences, negotiating contracts, or establishing business partnerships, a Business Visa (F Visa) is essential. This visa is valid for up to 90 days, allowing you to conduct your business activities efficiently.

Transit Visas (G Visas)
If your journey to Shanghai involves a stopover en route to another destination, a Transit Visa (G Visa) is required. This visa grants you permission to stay in Shanghai for up to 144 hours, ensuring a smooth transition during your travel itinerary.

Applying for a Visa
To obtain a visa for Shanghai, you should initiate the application process at a Chinese embassy or consulate in your home country. The application typically takes 3-5 business days, but it is advisable to apply well in advance of your trip, especially during peak travel seasons.

Passport Requirements
In addition to a valid visa, all travelers entering Shanghai must possess a valid passport with at least six months of remaining validity beyond the intended date

of departure from China. Your passport should also have at least two blank visa pages to accommodate the necessary stamps and endorsements.

Considerations
Biometric Data Collection: Certain Chinese visa applications require applicants to provide biometric data, including fingerprints and facial scans. This process is typically conducted at the embassy or consulate where you are applying for your visa.

Visa Extensions: If you need to extend your visa while in China, you can do so at a local exit-entry administration bureau.

Visa-Free Transit: Citizens of select countries with valid onward travel documents can transit through Shanghai without a visa for up to 72 hours.

Visa-Free Entry: Citizens of certain countries with valid passports can enter Shanghai without a visa for up to 15 days.

For the most up-to-date information on visa and passport requirements for Shanghai, please consult the official website of the Chinese embassy or consulate in your home country.

Currency Exchange

Shanghai, the bustling metropolis of China, operates on the Chinese Yuan (CNY), commonly referred to as the Renminbi (RMB). The Yuan is divided into 10 jiao (角) and 100 fen (分). The currency comes in denominations of coins (1, 5, and 10 jiao, 1 Yuan) and banknotes (1, 5, 10, 20, 50, 100 Yuan).

Currency Exchange Rates

The value of the Yuan fluctuates against other currencies based on market conditions and economic factors. However, to provide a general guideline, as of July 2023, the approximate exchange rates are:

- 1 USD = 6.67 CNY
- 1 EUR = 7.00 CNY
- 1 GBP = 8.70 CNY
- 1 AUD = 5.00 CNY
- 1 JPY = 4.90 CNY

Currency Exchange Options

Travelers to Shanghai have several options for exchanging their foreign currency into Yuan:

Banks: Banks offer competitive exchange rates and are widely available throughout the city. However, it's advisable to compare rates and fees before exchanging at a bank.

Currency Exchange Bureaus: These specialized bureaus offer convenient locations and quick exchange services. However, their rates may vary depending on the location and currency being exchanged.

Hotels: Most hotels provide currency exchange services for their guests, but the rates may not be as favorable as banks or exchange bureaus.

Airports: Currency exchange counters are available at both Shanghai Pudong International Airport (PVG) and Shanghai Hongqiao International Airport (SHA). However, the rates may be slightly higher than in the city.

Tips for Currency Exchange
- Avoid Airport Exchange: If possible, avoid exchanging currency at the airport as the rates tend to be less favorable.
- Compare Rates: Before exchanging currency, compare rates at different banks, exchange bureaus, and hotels to find the best deal.

- Inquire About Fees: Ask about any applicable fees or commissions before exchanging currency.
- Keep Exchange Receipts: Retain exchange receipts for any future transactions or inquiries.
- Avoid Large Amounts: Exchange only the amount of Yuan you need for immediate use and avoid carrying large amounts of cash.
- Consider Using a Debit or Credit Card: Most establishments in Shanghai accept major debit and credit cards, reducing the need for large cash withdrawals.

By following these tips and understanding the currency exchange process, travelers can ensure a smooth and cost-effective financial experience while exploring the captivating city of Shanghai.

Transportation to and from Shanghai

Here is a detailed guide to transportation to and from Shanghai:

Arriving in Shanghai
Shanghai boasts two major international airports, Shanghai Pudong International Airport (PVG) and

Shanghai Hongqiao International Airport (SHA), catering to both domestic and international flights. Both airports offer efficient connections to downtown Shanghai via various transportation options.

From Shanghai Pudong International Airport (PVG)
Maglev Train: The Shanghai Maglev Train, the fastest commercial train in the world, connects PVG to Longyang Road Station in just 7 minutes.

Metro Line 2: Metro Line 2 offers a direct connection from PVG to downtown Shanghai, with stops at major attractions and business districts.

Taxi: Taxis are readily available outside the airport terminals. The journey to downtown Shanghai takes approximately 30-45 minutes, depending on traffic conditions.

Bus: Airport shuttle buses provide a budget-friendly option, connecting PVG to major transportation hubs and hotels in the city.

From Shanghai Hongqiao International Airport (SHA)
Metro Lines 2 and 10: Metro Lines 2 and 10 provide direct connections from SHA to downtown Shanghai, with stops at various landmarks and business centers.

Taxi: Taxis are readily available outside the airport terminals. The journey to downtown Shanghai takes approximately 20-30 minutes, depending on traffic conditions.

Bus: Airport shuttle buses offer a budget-friendly option, connecting SHA to major transportation hubs and hotels in the city.

Transportation Within Shanghai
Shanghai's extensive and efficient transportation network makes it easy to navigate the city with ease. A variety of options, including the metro, buses, taxis, and ride-hailing services, are readily available.

Metro: Shanghai's metro system is one of the most extensive in the world, with 16 lines covering all major districts and attractions. It is a convenient and affordable way to get around the city.

Buses: Shanghai's bus network provides comprehensive coverage, with over 1,000 routes connecting various neighborhoods and suburbs.

Taxis: Taxis are readily available throughout Shanghai, offering a comfortable and direct way to travel.

Ride-hailing Services: Popular ride-hailing apps like Didi Chuxing and Uber operate in Shanghai, providing convenient and cashless transportation options.

Transportation Options to Nearby Destinations
From Shanghai, travelers can easily access nearby destinations via various transportation modes:

High-speed Trains: Shanghai's high-speed rail network connects to major cities across China, offering fast and convenient travel options.

Intercity Buses: Intercity buses provide a budget-friendly alternative for shorter distances, connecting Shanghai to nearby towns and cities.

Ferry: Ferry services are available from Shanghai to nearby islands and coastal destinations, offering a scenic and relaxing mode of travel.

By understanding the various transportation options available, travelers can seamlessly navigate Shanghai and explore the surrounding regions with ease.

Accommodation Options in Shanghai

Shanghai, a captivating city brimming with cultural allure and modern sophistication, offers a diverse array of accommodation options tailored to every traveler's needs and preferences. Here are some recommendation for the best stays in Shanghai:

Luxury Stays

Shanghai offers a plethora of luxurious accommodation options that cater to the discerning traveler's every desire.

1. The Peninsula Shanghai: Epitome of Timeless Elegance
- Location: 32 The Bund, 200010, China
- **Price:** Starting from $600 per night

Nestled on the legendary Bund waterfront, The Peninsula Shanghai exudes an aura of timeless elegance and grandeur. This iconic hotel is renowned for its lavish accommodations, world-class dining experiences, and impeccable service, ensuring an unparalleled stay in the heart of Shanghai's historic district.

Features:
- Panoramic city views from many rooms
- Award-winning restaurants, including Sir Elly's and The Peninsula Spa by ESPA
- Exquisite Art Deco interiors
- Serene spa offering a range of rejuvenating treatments
- Personalized butler service for every guest

2. Fairmont Peace Hotel On the Bund: A Glimpse into Shanghai's Golden Age
- Location: 20 The Bund, 200010, China
- Price: Starting from $500 per night

Steeped in history and architectural splendor, the Fairmont Peace Hotel On the Bund seamlessly blends heritage with modern luxury. This iconic hotel, once frequented by luminaries like Charlie Chaplin and Noel Coward, offers a captivating journey through Shanghai's rich past.

Features:
- Art Deco architecture and interiors reminiscent of Shanghai's golden age

- Iconic Jazz Bar 88, a tribute to the city's vibrant jazz scene
- Prime location for exploring the Bund and surrounding attractions
- Award-winning cuisine, including M on the Bund and Dragon Phoenix
- Personalized service tailored to individual preferences

3. The Puli Hotel And Spa: Tranquility amidst the Urban Buzz

- Location: 333 Huangpi Road, Shanghai, China, 200005
- Price: Starting from $400 per night

Situated in the charming former French Concession, The Puli Hotel And Spa offers a tranquil retreat amidst the bustling city. This elegant hotel, inspired by Shanghai's rich history and culture, provides a haven for relaxation and rejuvenation.

Features:
- Art Deco-inspired design with contemporary touches
- Serenity Garden, a tranquil oasis in the heart of Shanghai
- Award-winning culinary experiences at The Puli Bar & Grill

- Chuan Spa, offering traditional Chinese therapies and wellness treatments
- Personalized service with a focus on guest well-being

These luxurious havens in Shanghai promise an unforgettable stay, catering to the discerning traveler's every need and desire. Whether seeking timeless elegance, a glimpse into Shanghai's golden age, or tranquility amidst the urban buzz, these exquisite accommodations will provide a memorable experience in the heart of this captivating metropolis.

Mid-Range Options

Shanghai offers a diverse array of mid-range accommodation options that cater to a wide range of travelers seeking a balance between comfort, convenience, and value. These establishments provide stylish accommodations, attentive service, and prime locations, making them ideal for both leisure travelers and business professionals.

1. Atour Hotel Shanghai Center Lujiazui: Modern Comfort in the Heart of Pudong
- Location: 1308 Pudong South Road, Shanghai 200120, China
- Price: Starting from $200 per night

Conveniently located in the heart of the Pudong financial district, Atour Hotel Shanghai Center Lujiazui provides stylish and comfortable accommodations at an attractive price. This modern hotel offers a seamless blend of business-friendly amenities and leisure facilities, catering to the diverse needs of its guests.

Features:
- Modern design and contemporary furnishings
- Convenient location for business meetings and conferences
- Sky Lounge with stunning city views
- Well-equipped fitness center
- Attentive and personalized service

2. Broadway Mansions Hotel - Bund: A Blend of Heritage and Contemporary Style
- Location: 555 Zhongshan East Road, Shanghai, China, 200002
- Price: Starting from $150 per night

Situated on the iconic Bund waterfront, Broadway Mansions Hotel - Bund offers a unique blend of heritage and contemporary style. This charming hotel seamlessly integrates the Bund's rich history with modern amenities, providing a memorable Shanghai experience.

Features:
- Heritage architecture with modern touches
- Riverfront views overlooking the Bund and Pudong skyline
- Proximity to Shanghai's iconic landmarks and cultural attractions
- Elegant dining options, including The Exchange Restaurant and The Broadway Bar
- Personalized service with a focus on guest satisfaction

3. Capella Shanghai, Jian Ye Li: A Serene Retreat in the Former French Concession
- Location: 120 Fenchang Road, Xuhui District, Shanghai 200233, China
- Price: Starting from $300 per night

Nestled within the tranquil Jian Ye Li complex, Capella Shanghai offers a refined and exclusive retreat in the heart of the city. This elegant hotel provides a haven for discerning travelers seeking a truly exceptional experience, combining modern luxury with the tranquility of traditional Chinese courtyard architecture.

Features:
- Exquisite Art Deco design and luxurious interiors

- Private courtyards and gardens for tranquility
- Capella Culinair, a Michelin-starred restaurant offering exquisite dining
- Auriga Spa, providing a range of rejuvenating treatments
- Personalized service with an emphasis on guest privacy and exclusivity

Budget Options

Shanghai offers a diverse array of budget-friendly accommodation options that cater to travelers seeking affordable and comfortable lodging without sacrificing convenience or quality.

1. Shanghai Fish Inn East Nanjing Road: Convenience and Comfort in the Heart of Shopping District

- Location: 222 East Nanjing Road, Huangpu District, Shanghai 200002, China
- Price: Starting from $50 per night

Situated in the heart of Nanjing Road shopping district, Shanghai Fish Inn East Nanjing Road offers affordable and convenient accommodations. This clean and comfortable hotel provides easy access to a plethora of shops, restaurants, and transportation options, making it an ideal base for exploring Shanghai's bustling commercial center.

Features:
- Clean and comfortable rooms with basic amenities
- Convenient location for shopping, dining, and sightseeing
- Proximity to metro stations and public transportation
- Friendly and helpful staff
- Affordable rates suitable for budget travelers

2. Sheraton Shanghai Pudong Hotel & Residences: Modern Comfort at a Reasonable Price
- Location: 1000 Century Avenue, Pudong New Area, Shanghai 200120, China
- Price: Starting from $80 per night

Situated in the Pudong financial district, Sheraton Shanghai Pudong Hotel & Residences offers stylish and comfortable accommodations at a reasonable price. This modern hotel provides a blend of business-friendly amenities and leisure facilities, catering to both business and leisure travelers.

Features:
- Modern furnishings and amenities in all rooms

- Riverfront views overlooking the Huangpu River
- Convenient access to business hubs and transportation
- Well-equipped fitness center and swimming pool
- Attentive and personalized service

3. Grand Hyatt Shanghai: Luxury at an Affordable Price Point

- Location: 88 Century Avenue, Pudong New Area, Shanghai
- Price: Starting from $100 per night

Located in the Pudong financial district, Grand Hyatt Shanghai offers luxurious accommodations with stunning city views at an affordable price point. This elegant hotel provides a haven for discerning travelers seeking a balance between comfort, convenience, and value.

Features:
- Spacious rooms with modern furnishings and amenities
- Panoramic city views from many rooms
- World-class dining options, including The Grill and M on the Bund
- Extensive spa and wellness facilities

- Personalized service with a focus on guest satisfaction

Booking Tips & Websites

Booking Tips

Plan ahead: Popular hotels and hostels in Shanghai can book up quickly, especially during peak seasons. It is advisable to book your accommodations well in advance, especially if you are traveling during Chinese holidays or major events.

Consider your budget: Shanghai offers a wide range of accommodation options to suit all budgets, from luxury hotels to budget-friendly hostels. Decide on your budget before you start searching for hotels, and consider factors such as location, amenities, and reviews.

Read reviews: Before booking a hotel, take some time to read reviews from other guests. This can give you valuable insights into the hotel's facilities, service, and overall experience.

Compare prices: Use online hotel booking websites to compare prices for different hotels. Consider booking directly with the hotel, as they may offer special promotions or packages.

Be flexible with your dates: If you are flexible with your travel dates, you may be able to find better deals on hotels. Try searching for hotels on weekdays or during the off-season.

Booking Websites

Here are some popular websites for booking hotels in Shanghai:

Ctrip: Ctrip is one of the largest online travel agencies in China, offering a wide range of hotels and hostels in Shanghai. It is available in both English and Chinese.

Fliggy: Fliggy is another popular Chinese online travel agency that offers a wide range of hotels and hostels in Shanghai. It is also available in both English and Chinese.

Agoda: Agoda is a Singapore-based online travel agency that specializes in Asian hotels. It offers a wide range of hotels and hostels in Shanghai, and its website is available in multiple languages, including English.

Booking.com: Booking.com is a global online travel agency that offers a wide range of hotels and hostels in Shanghai. Its website is available in multiple languages, including English.

HotelsCombined: HotelsCombined is a metasearch engine that aggregates prices from various online travel agencies to find the best deals on hotels. It is a useful tool for comparing prices and finding the best deals.

These booking websites offer a variety of search filters to help you narrow down your options, such as location, price, amenities, and guest ratings. You can also read reviews from other guests to get a sense of the hotel's atmosphere and amenities.

Once you have found a hotel that you like, you can book your room directly on the website. Be sure to read the cancellation policy carefully before you book, and make sure you understand the payment terms.

What to Pack for a Trip to Shanghai

Here is a comprehensive guide on what to pack for a trip to Shanghai, covering all essential items and considering seasonal variations:

Essentials

Passport and visa (if required): Ensure your passport is valid for at least six months beyond your travel dates and obtain a visa if necessary.

Travel documents: Carry copies of your passport, travel insurance, and itinerary for easy access.

Currency exchange: Bring sufficient Chinese Yuan (CNY) for your expenses, as some places may not accept foreign cards.

Electronic devices and chargers: Pack your phone, camera, chargers, and any other electronic devices you may need. Consider a universal adapter if necessary.

Medicine: Pack any prescription medication you may require, along with over-the-counter remedies for common ailments.

Toiletries: Bring your essential toiletries, including shampoo, conditioner, soap, toothbrush, toothpaste, and sunscreen.

Clothing:

Spring (March-May): Pack light jackets, shirts, pants, and comfortable shoes.

Summer (June-August): Pack light and breathable clothing like t-shirts, shorts, skirts, and sandals.

Autumn (September-November): Bring a mix of light and medium-weight clothing, including long-sleeved shirts, jackets, and light sweaters.

Winter (December-February): Pack warm layers like sweaters, coats, hats, gloves, and scarves.

Considerations
Luggage: Choose luggage that is lightweight, durable, and fits your travel needs. Consider a backpack for easy maneuverability.

Day bag: Pack a small day bag for carrying essentials during your outings.

Footwear: Pack comfortable shoes for walking and exploring the city. Consider bringing a pair of rain shoes in case of inclement weather.

Cultural sensitivities: Pack modest clothing for visiting temples and religious sites.

Entertainment: Bring books, magazines, or a portable music player for downtime.

Gifts and souvenirs: Consider packing small gifts for friends or family you may meet during your trip.

Packing Tips
- Roll your clothes: Rolling clothes saves space and helps prevent wrinkles.
- Utilize packing cubes: Packing cubes organize your belongings and maximize space in your luggage.
- Wear your bulkiest items: Wear your heavy shoes and jackets to save packing space.
- Leave room for souvenirs: Don't pack your luggage to the brim; leave space for souvenirs you may purchase during your trip.

Chapter 2: Exploring Shanghai's Neighborhoods

Unveil the captivating tapestry of Shanghai's neighborhoods, each with its own distinct personality and allure. Discover the captivating fusion of colonial grandeur and modern marvels along the Bund, wander through the enchanting lanes of the erstwhile French Concession, immerse yourself in the revitalized Xintiandi district, explore the upscale allure of Jing'an, and marvel at the futuristic panorama of Pudong.

The Bund

Along the western bank of the Huangpu River, where the past and present intertwine, lies the Bund, an iconic waterfront promenade that epitomizes Shanghai's heritage and modernity. Step into a realm where grand colonial-era buildings stand as testaments to the city's illustrious past, their facades adorned with intricate details and exuding an aura of timeless elegance.

Distance: The Bund stretches for approximately 1.5 kilometers along the Huangpu River, from Waibaidu Bridge to Nanpu Bridge, making it easily accessible from various parts of the city.

How to Get There:
Subway: Take Metro Line 2 to East Nanjing Road Station or Bund Station, both conveniently located within walking distance of the Bund's attractions.

Taxi: Taxis are readily available throughout Shanghai. Simply provide the taxi driver with the address of your destination, which can be 'The Bund, Shanghai' or a specific landmark within the Bund area.

Bus: Multiple bus routes serve the Bund area, including Bus 14, 42, 751, and 960. These buses provide a convenient and affordable option for reaching the Bund.

Must-See Attractions and Activities:
Admire the Architectural Splendor: Stroll along the Bund promenade and marvel at the iconic colonial-era buildings, including the Shanghai Customs House, the Bank of China Building, and the Peace Hotel.

Capture Panoramic Views: Climb to the top of the Oriental Pearl Tower or the Shanghai World Financial Center for breathtaking panoramic views of the city skyline and the Bund.

Indulge in Culinary Delights: Savor delectable cuisine at renowned restaurants like M on the Bund, Sir Elly's, or The Peninsula Shanghai, offering a blend of international and Shanghainese flavors.

Enjoy Cultural Experiences: Immerse yourself in Shanghai's rich culture by visiting the Shanghai Museum of Art or the Bund Historical Museum.

Take a Huangpu River Cruise: Embark on a leisurely Huangpu River cruise to admire the Bund's architectural grandeur from a unique perspective.

Visiting Tips:
- Best Time to Visit: The Bund is particularly charming during the day when the architecture is illuminated by sunlight. However, the evening offers a mesmerizing spectacle of city lights and river reflections.
- Photography Tips: Capture stunning shots of the Bund's iconic landmarks from various angles, including from the riverbank, across the Huangpu River, or from rooftops.
- Dining Reservations: If you plan to dine at one of the Bund's popular restaurants, consider making reservations in advance, especially during peak hours.

The French Concession

Nestled amidst the bustling heart of Shanghai, the French Concession emerges as an oasis of tranquility, a charming haven where tree-lined avenues, quaint cafes, and Art Deco architecture transport visitors to an era of elegance and refinement.

Distance: The French Concession is located in the Huangpu District, covering an area of approximately 8.3 square kilometers. It is easily accessible from various parts of the city by subway, taxi, or bus.

How to Get There:
Subway: Take Metro Line 1 to Fuxing Road Station, Metro Line 2 to Xujiahui Station, or Metro Line 7 to Changshu Road Station, all located within the French Concession's boundaries.

Taxi: Taxis are readily available throughout Shanghai. Simply provide the taxi driver with the address of your destination, such as a specific landmark or street within the French Concession.

Bus: Multiple bus routes serve the French Concession area, including Bus 20, 44, 48, 55, 71, and 960. These buses provide a convenient and affordable option for reaching the French Concession.

Must-See Attractions and Activities:
Wander through Fuxing Middle Road: Stroll along the iconic Fuxing Middle Road, lined with charming cafes, boutiques, and Art Deco buildings, and immerse yourself in the neighborhood's unique ambiance.

Explore Former Residences: Discover the captivating history of the French Concession by visiting the former residences of luminaries like Soong Ching Ling, the widow of Sun Yat-sen, and Zhou Enlai, the first Premier of the People's Republic of China.

Admire Art Deco Architecture: Take a leisurely walk and admire the Art Deco architecture that graces the streets of the French Concession, capturing the essence of Shanghai's architectural heritage.

Indulge in Culinary Delights: Savor a taste of Shanghai's culinary scene by dining at a traditional Shanghainese restaurant or indulging in international cuisines at the many upscale eateries within the French Concession.

Experience Local Markets: Immerse yourself in the vibrant atmosphere of the French Concession's local markets, such as the Fuxing Road Antique Market or the Tianzifang Market, and discover hidden gems and authentic Shanghai experiences.

Additional Tips:
- Best Time to Visit: The French Concession is particularly charming during the day when the tree-lined avenues provide a welcome respite from the city's hustle and bustle. However, the evenings offer a delightful ambiance with the twinkling lights of cafes and boutiques casting a warm glow.
- Photography Tips: Capture the essence of the French Concession's unique charm by photographing its Art Deco architecture, quaint cafes, and vibrant street scenes.
- Language Assistance: Although English is becoming increasingly common in Shanghai, carrying a phrasebook or using translation apps can be helpful in navigating the French Concession and communicating with local vendors.

Xintiandi

In the heart of Shanghai, where the past and present converge, lies Xintiandi, a captivating district that seamlessly blends traditional Shikumen architecture with modern urban sensibilities. This vibrant enclave offers a unique blend of cultural attractions, upscale dining options, and trendy boutiques, making it a must-visit destination for both leisure and business travelers.

Distance: Xintiandi is conveniently located in the Huangpu District, just a short distance from the iconic Bund and the Nanjing Road shopping district. The district is easily accessible by subway, taxi, or bus.

How to Get There:
Subway: Take Metro Line 1 to Huangpi Road Station or Metro Line 10 to Nanjing Road Station, both located within walking distance of Xintiandi's main attractions.

Taxi: Taxis are readily available throughout Shanghai. Simply provide the taxi driver with the address of your destination, such as a specific restaurant, bar, or attraction within Xintiandi.

Bus: Multiple bus routes serve the Xintiandi area, including Bus 9, 24, 37, 42, 48, and 71. These buses provide a convenient and affordable option for reaching Xintiandi.

Must-See Attractions and Activities:
Stroll through Shikumen Alleys: Immerse yourself in the charm of Xintiandi's labyrinthine alleyways, lined with traditional Shikumen houses that have been revitalized and transformed into trendy shops, restaurants, and bars.

Explore Cultural Venues: Delve into Shanghai's rich cultural heritage by visiting the Shanghai Museum of Art, the Xintiandi Style Museum, or the Shanghai Dramatic Arts Centre, each offering a unique perspective on the city's cultural tapestry.

Indulge in Culinary Delights: Savor a taste of Shanghai's diverse culinary scene by dining at one of Xintiandi's numerous restaurants, offering everything from traditional Shanghainese cuisine to international flavors.

Enjoy Live Entertainment: Catch a captivating performance at the Xintiandi Live Theatre, renowned for its theatrical productions and musical performances.

Relax at a Rooftop Bar: Unwind with a refreshing cocktail or indulge in a leisurely afternoon tea at one of Xintiandi's rooftop bars, offering panoramic views of the city skyline and the Huangpu River.

Visiting Tips:
- Best Time to Visit: Xintiandi is particularly enchanting during the evening hours when the Shikumen alleys are illuminated by a warm glow and the district comes alive with vibrant energy.
- Photography Tips: Capture the essence of Xintiandi's unique character by photographing its traditional Shikumen architecture, lively street scenes, and captivating cultural attractions.
- Language Assistance: While English is becoming increasingly common in Shanghai, carrying a phrasebook or using translation apps can be helpful in communicating with local vendors or navigating the district's smaller establishments.

Jing'an

In the heart of Shanghai's bustling commercial district, Jing'an emerges as an oasis of luxury and refinement, a neighborhood where elegance and sophistication intertwine with the city's vibrant energy. Home to upscale shopping malls, Michelin-starred restaurants, and world-class hotels, Jing'an epitomizes Shanghai's modern allure and caters to discerning travelers seeking a taste of refined luxury.

Distance: Jing'an is conveniently located in the Huangpu District, adjacent to the French Concession and just a short distance from the iconic Bund. The district is easily accessible by subway, taxi, or bus.

How to Get There:
Subway: Take Metro Line 2 to Jing'an Temple Station, Metro Line 7 to Changshu Road Station, or Metro Line 13 to Xujiahui Station, all located within the heart of Jing'an's attractions.

Taxi: Taxis are readily available throughout Shanghai. Simply provide the taxi driver with the address of your destination, such as a specific hotel, shopping mall, or restaurant in Jing'an.

Bus: Multiple bus routes serve the Jing'an area, including Bus 14, 42, 44, 48, 71, and 960. These buses provide a convenient and affordable option for reaching Jing'an.

Must-See Attractions and Activities:
Indulge in Luxury Shopping: Embark on a shopping spree at Jing'an's upscale malls, such as the Jing'an Kerry Centre or the Shanghai Centre, where you'll find a curated selection of international luxury brands and high-end fashion.

Savor Culinary Delights: Experience the pinnacle of fine dining at Jing'an's Michelin-starred restaurants, offering exquisite cuisine and impeccable service.

Immerse in Art and Culture: Visit the Jing'an Art Center or the Jing'an Temple, a serene oasis amidst the urban buzz, to appreciate the district's vibrant art scene and rich cultural heritage.

Enjoy a Luxurious Stay: Pamper yourself at Jing'an's world-class hotels, such as the Jing'an Shangri-La or the Capella Shanghai, where you'll be treated to opulent accommodations, personalized service, and exceptional amenities.

Stroll through Jing'an Park: Take a leisurely stroll through Jing'an Park, a tranquil green space offering a respite from the city's hustle and bustle, and enjoy its lush gardens, serene ponds, and picturesque bridges.

Visiting Tips:
- Best Time to Visit: Jing'an is particularly charming during the evening hours when the streets are illuminated by the glow of upscale boutiques and restaurants, creating an ambiance of luxury and sophistication.
- Photography Tips: Capture the essence of Jing'an's luxurious character by photographing its elegant architecture, stylish boutiques, and inviting cafes.
- Language Assistance: Although English is becoming increasingly common in Shanghai, carrying a phrasebook or using translation apps can be helpful in communicating with hotel staff, shop assistants, or restaurant personnel.

Pudong

Across the Huangpu River from Shanghai's historic Bund, Pudong district emerges as a captivating metropolis of the future, a testament to human ingenuity and innovation. Soaring skyscrapers pierce the sky, each a beacon of technological advancement, while expansive boulevards weave through the district, pulsating with the energy of a thriving global hub. Pudong is a symphony of modern marvels, where urban grandeur meets cutting-edge technology, offering a glimpse into the future of urban living.

Distance: Pudong is conveniently located across the Huangpu River from the city center, easily accessible by subway, ferry, or taxi. The district spans a vast area, encompassing both Lujiazui, the financial hub, and the more traditional Qiantan area.

How to Get There:
Subway: Take Metro Line 2 to Lujiazui Station or Metro Line 9 to Century Avenue Station, both located in the heart of Lujiazui's financial district. For Qiantan, take Metro Line 2 to Dongchang Road Station or Metro Line 6 to Shangcheng Road Station.

Ferry: Take the Huangpu River ferry from the Bund to Pudong's Yichang Road Ferry Terminal or Yu Garden Ferry Terminal, offering a scenic and relaxing option for crossing the river.

Taxi: Taxis are readily available throughout Shanghai. Simply provide the taxi driver with the address of your destination, such as a specific landmark, hotel, or shopping mall in Pudong.

Must-See Attractions and Activities:
Ascend the Oriental Pearl Tower: Marvel at the panoramic views of Shanghai from the Oriental Pearl Tower, an iconic landmark that has become a symbol of the city's modernity.

Explore the Shanghai World Financial Center: Witness the architectural marvel of the Shanghai World Financial Center, adorned with a unique circular opening at its apex, resembling a giant eye gazing upon the city.

Admire the Shanghai Tower: Experience the sheer grandeur of the Shanghai Tower, the tallest building in China, and enjoy breathtaking views from its observation deck.

Wander through Lujiazui Financial District: Stroll along the bustling streets of Lujiazui, the heart of Shanghai's financial district, and admire the towering skyscrapers that define the city's skyline.

Immerse in Cutting-edge Technology: Explore the Shanghai Science and Technology Museum and the Shanghai Museum of Natural History to delve into the world of innovation and scientific advancements.

Visiting Tips:
- Best Time to Visit: Pudong is particularly captivating at night when the skyscrapers are illuminated, creating a mesmerizing spectacle of lights and shadows.
- Photography Tips: Capture the futuristic allure of Pudong by photographing its towering skyscrapers, intricate architectural details, and vibrant street scenes.
- Language Assistance: While English is becoming increasingly common in Shanghai, carrying a phrasebook or using translation apps can be helpful in communicating with locals and navigating smaller establishments.

Chapter 3: Must-See Attractions in Shanghai

Delve into the heart of Shanghai, where captivating landmarks await your exploration. Embark on a journey through time and culture, discovering icons that embody the city's rich heritage, vibrant spirit, and modern innovations. Ascend to the dizzying heights of the Oriental Pearl Tower, immerse yourself in the vast artistic treasures of the Shanghai Museum, wander through the tranquil haven of Yu Garden, and marvel at the exquisite sculptures of the Jade Buddha Temple. Embrace the unique subterranean experience of the Bund Sightseeing Tunnel, gliding beneath the Huangpu River to witness Shanghai's captivating skyline from a new perspective. Prepare to be captivated by the enchanting tapestry of Shanghai's must-see attractions.

The Oriental Pearl Tower

Amidst the bustling metropolis of Shanghai, the Oriental Pearl Tower stands as a beacon of innovation and architectural grandeur. Piercing the sky with its distinctive silhouette, this iconic landmark has become synonymous with the city's rapid development and unwavering spirit.

Location:
Situated in the heart of Pudong, Shanghai's financial district, the Oriental Pearl Tower is easily accessible by various modes of transportation. By subway, take Metro Line 2 to Lujiazui Station or Metro Line 9 to Century Avenue Station. Taxis are readily available throughout the city, and simply provide the address as "Oriental Pearl Tower, Pudong, Shanghai."

Prices:
Ticket prices for the Oriental Pearl Tower vary depending on the specific observation deck and the day of the week. General admission tickets for adults range from CNY 160 (approximately USD 23) to CNY 220 (approximately USD 32), while children's tickets are priced between CNY 80 (approximately USD 12) and CNY 110 (approximately USD 16).

Must-See Highlights:
Space Capsule: Ascend to the Space Capsule observation deck, located at a height of 350 meters (1,148 feet), and enjoy breathtaking panoramic views of Shanghai's sprawling cityscape.

Sightseeing Tunnel: Embark on a thrilling journey through the Sightseeing Tunnel, a subterranean passage that offers unique perspectives of the Oriental Pearl Tower and the Huangpu River.

Shanghai City History Exhibition: Delve into Shanghai's rich history and cultural heritage at the Shanghai City History Exhibition, located in the tower's base.

Revolving Restaurant: Indulge in a culinary experience at the Revolving Restaurant, offering exquisite cuisine amidst panoramic views of the city.

Visiting Tips:
- Best Time to Visit: For the most captivating views, visit the Oriental Pearl Tower during the day when the city is illuminated by sunlight. However, the tower also offers a mesmerizing spectacle of city lights and river reflections in the evenings.
- Photography Tips: Capture stunning shots of the Oriental Pearl Tower's unique architecture from various angles, including from the observation decks, the surrounding streets, or from across the Huangpu River.
- Pre-Booking Tickets: Consider pre-booking your tickets online or through authorized agents

to avoid long queues, especially during peak seasons.

The Shanghai Museum

Nestled in the heart of Shanghai's People's Square, the Shanghai Museum stands as a majestic repository of China's rich cultural heritage. Spanning over 700,000 years of history, its vast collection of over 120,000 artifacts encompasses a diverse array of artistic and cultural expressions, offering a captivating glimpse into the nation's past.

Location:
Conveniently located in the Huangpu District, the Shanghai Museum is easily accessible by various modes of transportation. By subway, take Metro Line 1, 2, or 8 to People's Square Station and follow the signs to the museum. Taxis are readily available throughout the city, and simply provide the address as "Shanghai Museum, People's Square, Shanghai."

Admission and Hours:
General Admission: CNY 60 (approximately USD 9) for adults, CNY 30 (approximately USD 4) for

students and seniors, and free for children under 6 years old.

Opening Hours: 9:00 AM to 5:00 PM, Tuesday through Sunday (closed on Mondays).

Must-See Highlights:
Bronze Collection: Renowned for its extensive collection of bronzes, the Shanghai Museum showcases exquisite artifacts dating back to the Shang and Zhou dynasties, including ceremonial vessels, weapons, and sculptures.

Ceramic Collection: Immerse yourself in the world of Chinese ceramics, exploring a vast array of porcelain, pottery, and stoneware from various periods, each piece showcasing intricate craftsmanship and artistic mastery.

Calligraphy and Painting Collection: Delve into the evolution of Chinese calligraphy and painting, admiring masterpieces by renowned artists from various dynasties, showcasing the elegance and expressive power of these art forms.

Jade Collection: Marvel at the exquisite beauty of jade, a revered material in Chinese culture, with artifacts ranging from delicate jewelry to intricate carvings and sculptures.

Ancient Sculpture Gallery: Discover the artistry and craftsmanship of ancient Chinese sculptors, exploring a diverse array of sculptures from various periods, depicting deities, mythical creatures, and historical figures.

Visiting Tips:
- Audio Guides: Enhance your museum experience by renting an audio guide, available in multiple languages, providing detailed insights into the exhibits and their historical context.
- Special Exhibitions: Check the museum's website or inquire at the information desk for details on any special exhibitions that may be running during your visit.
- Museum Dining: Enjoy a leisurely meal at the museum's restaurant, offering a selection of Chinese and Western cuisines.
- Museum Shop: Browse through the museum shop for a wide range of souvenirs, including replicas of artifacts, books, and traditional Chinese handicrafts.

The Yu Garden

In the heart of Shanghai's bustling metropolis, nestled amidst towering skyscrapers and bustling streets, lies the Yu Garden, a tranquil oasis of verdant gardens, intricate architecture, and serene ponds. Stepping into this captivating realm is like embarking on a journey through time, transported to an era of emperors and scholars, where tranquility and harmony reign supreme.

Location:

Situated in the Huangpu District, the Yu Garden is easily accessible by various modes of transportation. By subway, take Metro Line 10 to Yuyuan Garden Station or Metro Line 8 to Yu Garden Station. Taxis are readily available throughout the city, and simply provide the address as "Yu Garden, Huangpu District, Shanghai."

Admission and Hours:

General Admission: CNY 40 (approximately USD 6) for adults, CNY 20 (approximately USD 3) for students and seniors, and free for children under 6 years old.

Opening Hours: 8:30 AM to 5:30 PM, daily.

Must-See Highlights:

Wanhua Chamber: Admire the exquisite architecture of the Wanhua Chamber, a two-story pavilion with intricate carvings and a tranquil courtyard.

Dianchun Hall: Immerse yourself in the serene ambiance of the Dianchun Hall, surrounded by lush greenery and offering a glimpse into the garden's rich history.

Huijing Hall: Discover the beauty of traditional Chinese architecture in the Huijing Hall, adorned with intricate carvings and offering a tranquil space for contemplation.

Yuhua Hall: Marvel at the exquisite craftsmanship of the Yuhua Hall, a two-story pavilion with a unique octagonal design and intricate carvings.

Inner Garden: Wander through the Inner Garden, a secluded paradise of meandering pathways, koi ponds, and verdant foliage, offering a peaceful escape from the city's hustle and bustle.

Visiting Tips:
- Best Time to Visit: The Yu Garden is particularly enchanting during the spring and autumn seasons when the gardens are in full bloom.
- Photography Tips: Capture the garden's captivating beauty by photographing its intricate architecture, serene ponds, and vibrant flora.
- Language Assistance: While English is becoming increasingly common in Shanghai, carrying a phrasebook or using translation apps can be helpful in communicating with local vendors or navigating smaller establishments within the garden complex.

The Jade Buddha Temple

In the heart of Shanghai's bustling metropolis, nestled amidst towering skyscrapers and bustling streets, lies the Jade Buddha Temple, a sanctuary of serenity and spiritual enlightenment. Revered for its exquisite jade Buddha statues, this captivating temple offers a tranquil escape from the city's vibrant energy, inviting visitors to immerse themselves in the profound teachings of Buddhism.

Location:
Situated in the Huangpu District, the Jade Buddha Temple is easily accessible by various modes of transportation. By subway, take Metro Line 13 to Jiangsu Road Station or Metro Line 8 to Laoximen Station. Taxis are readily available throughout the city, and simply provide the address as "Jade Buddha Temple, Huangpu District, Shanghai."

Admission and Hours:
General Admission: CNY 20 (approximately USD 3) for adults, CNY 10 (approximately USD 1.5) for students and seniors, and free for children under 6 years old.

Opening Hours: 8:00 AM to 5:00 PM, daily.

Must-See Highlights:
Jade Buddha of Shakyamuni: Marvel at the centerpiece of the temple, the Jade Buddha of Shakyamuni, a colossal statue carved from a single piece of white jade.

Reclining Buddha Hall: Immerse yourself in the tranquility of the Reclining Buddha Hall, home to a serene statue of the Buddha resting on one side.

Mahavira Hall: Admire the grandeur of the Mahavira Hall, the temple's main sanctuary, adorned with intricate carvings and statues depicting Buddhist deities.

Dharma Drum Building: Experience the reverberating sound of the Dharma Drum, a sacred instrument believed to dispel evil and promote peace.

Vegetarian Dining: Savor a delectable vegetarian meal at the temple's restaurant, offering a taste of Buddhist cuisine.

Visiting Tips:
- Dress Code: Respect the temple's sanctity by dressing modestly, covering shoulders and knees.
- Respectful Conduct: Maintain a quiet and respectful demeanor while exploring the temple, avoiding loud conversations and disruptive behavior.
- Photography Restrictions: Photography is permitted in designated areas only, and be mindful not to disturb other visitors or disrupt religious ceremonies.
- Language Assistance: While English is becoming increasingly common in Shanghai,

carrying a phrasebook or using translation apps can be helpful in communicating with local vendors or navigating smaller establishments within the temple complex.

The Bund Sightseeing Tunnel

Beneath the bustling streets of Shanghai, amidst the ceaseless hum of urban life, lies a hidden gem – the Bund Sightseeing Tunnel. This unique subterranean passage offers an unprecedented perspective on the city's iconic waterfront, the Bund, transporting visitors on an immersive journey through time and space.

Location:
Situated in the Huangpu District, the Bund Sightseeing Tunnel is easily accessible by various modes of transportation. By subway, take Metro Line 2 to East Nanjing Road Station or Metro Line 10 to Yuyuan Garden Station. Taxis are readily available throughout the city, and simply provide the address as "Bund Sightseeing Tunnel, Huangpu District, Shanghai."

Admission and Hours:
General Admission: CNY 50 (approximately USD 7) for adults, CNY 25 (approximately USD 3.5) for

students and seniors, and free for children under 6 years old.

Opening Hours: 9:00 AM to 9:00 PM, daily.

Must-See Highlights:
Underwater Observation Deck: Ascend to the underwater observation deck and marvel at the panoramic views of the Huangpu River, watching as boats glide by and the bustling city lights reflect on the water's surface.

Multimedia Displays: Immerse yourself in the history and culture of Shanghai through interactive multimedia displays, showcasing the city's transformation from a humble fishing village to a global metropolis.

Magical Lighting Effects: Experience the captivating interplay of light and sound as you walk through the tunnel, creating a mesmerizing atmosphere that enhances the journey.

Bund Historical Museum: Delve into Shanghai's fascinating past at the Bund Historical Museum, located within the tunnel complex, offering insights into the city's rich heritage and cultural significance.

Sensory Tunnel: Engage your senses in the Sensory Tunnel, where a symphony of sounds, lights, and vibrations creates an immersive experience that stimulates the mind and body.

Visiting Tips:
- Best Time to Visit: The Bund Sightseeing Tunnel is particularly enchanting in the evenings when the lights of the Bund and the Huangpu River are reflected on the water's surface.
- Photography Tips: Capture stunning shots of the tunnel's unique architecture, the underwater observation deck's panoramic views, and the captivating multimedia displays.
- Language Assistance: Multilingual signs and audio guides are available to enhance the experience for non-Mandarin speakers.
- Accessibility: The tunnel is equipped with ramps and elevators, ensuring accessibility for visitors with disabilities.

Chapter 4: Shanghai's Culinary Scene

Embark on a culinary adventure through Shanghai's vibrant gastronomy, where flavors and aromas dance in harmony. Discover the essence of traditional Shanghainese cuisine, a symphony of sweet, savory, and umami flavors. Indulge in the tantalizing array of street food, a tapestry of flavors that captures the city's vibrant spirit. Explore the world of upscale dining, where culinary artistry meets refined ambiance. And immerse yourself in Shanghai's electrifying nightlife, where bars, clubs, and rooftop terraces pulsate with energy and offer a taste of the city's cosmopolitan flair.

Traditional Shanghainese Cuisine

Shanghai's culinary scene is a captivating tapestry of diverse flavors and culinary traditions, each reflecting the city's rich history and cultural influences. Among these, traditional Shanghainese cuisine stands out as a symphony of sweet, savory, and umami flavors, a testament to the region's culinary heritage and the ingenuity of its chefs.

Signature Dishes:

Xiao Long Bao: Experience the delicate artistry of Xiao Long Bao, succulent soup dumplings filled with a savory pork and broth filling that explodes with flavor in each bite.

Hong Shao Rou: Indulge in the rich and savory flavors of Hong Shao Rou, a braised pork belly dish that showcases the mastery of slow-cooking techniques.

Pan-Fried Pork Buns: Savor the crispy, golden perfection of Pan-Fried Pork Buns, a delightful street snack filled with a savory pork and vegetable filling.

Scallion Oil Noodles: Experience the simplicity and elegance of Scallion Oil Noodles, a comforting dish of thin noodles tossed in a fragrant scallion oil sauce.

Sweet and Sour Pork: Delight in the tangy and sweet flavors of Sweet and Sour Pork, a classic dish that showcases the versatility of Shanghainese cuisine.

Culinary Characteristics:

Balance of Flavors: Shanghainese cuisine emphasizes a delicate balance of sweet, savory, and umami flavors, creating a symphony of taste that is both harmonious and complex.

Fresh Ingredients: The emphasis on fresh, high-quality ingredients is paramount in Shanghainese cooking, ensuring that each dish showcases the natural flavors of its components.

Seasonality: Shanghainese cuisine honors the changing seasons, incorporating seasonal ingredients that reflect the freshness and vibrancy of nature's bounty.

Cooking Techniques: A variety of cooking techniques are employed in Shanghainese cuisine, including braising, stir-frying, steaming, and simmering, each method tailored to enhance the flavors of the ingredients.

Where to Experience Traditional Shanghainese Cuisine:
Nanxiang Mantou Dian: Renowned for its Xiao Long Bao, Nanxiang Mantou Dian is a must-visit for any food enthusiast exploring Shanghai's culinary scene.

Lao You Ji: Immerse yourself in the authentic flavors of traditional Shanghainese cuisine at Lao You Ji, a family-run restaurant that has been serving up delectable dishes for generations.

Fu Chun Xiao Long: Enjoy the delicate artistry of Xiao Long Bao at Fu Chun Xiao Long, a popular spot among locals and tourists alike.
Shanghai Grandmother's Kitchen: Experience the warmth and hospitality of a home-style Shanghainese dining experience at Shanghai Grandmother's Kitchen.

Chunfeng Deji Restaurant: Discover the hidden gem of Chunfeng Deji Restaurant, a traditional Shanghainese eatery tucked away in a local neighborhood.

Tips:
- Embrace the Local Experience: Venture beyond tourist hotspots and seek out authentic Shanghainese restaurants frequented by locals to truly immerse yourself in the city's culinary culture.
- Mind Your Manners: Be mindful of local dining etiquette, such as using chopsticks correctly and sharing dishes communally.
- Savor the Experience: Take your time to savor the flavors and aromas of each dish,

appreciating the culinary artistry that goes into Shanghainese cuisine.

Street Food in Shanghai

Shanghai's vibrant street food scene is a captivating tapestry of flavors, aromas, and cultural experiences, offering a glimpse into the city's dynamic spirit and culinary ingenuity. From bustling night markets to hidden alleyways, the city's streets transform into a culinary wonderland, where tantalizing aromas entice passersby and traditional dishes are prepared with a practiced finesse.

Signature Street Food Delights:
Shengjianbao: Experience the crispy perfection of Shengjianbao, pan-fried pork buns with a juicy, savory filling that bursts with flavor in each bite.

Congyoubing: Indulge in the savory goodness of Congyoubing, scallion pancakes that are crispy on the outside and soft and fluffy on the inside.

Xiaolongbao: Savor the delicate artistry of Xiaolongbao, soup dumplings filled with a pork and broth filling that explode with flavor.

Jianbing: Enjoy a savory and satisfying Jianbing, a crepe-like dish filled with eggs, vegetables, and various toppings.

Roujiamo: Indulge in the hearty flavors of Roujiamo, a braised pork sandwich that is a popular street food staple.

Must-Visit Street Food Markets:
Wulumuqin Street: Immerse yourself in the vibrant atmosphere of Wulumuqin Street, a bustling night market teeming with food vendors offering a diverse array of street food delights.

Changshu Road Food Market: Explore the authentic flavors of Changshu Road Food Market, a local favorite offering a wide variety of traditional Shanghainese street food.

Dongtai Road Food Market: Discover the hidden gems of Dongtai Road Food Market, a lesser-known market offering a taste of local delicacies and hidden culinary treasures.

South Xizang Road Food Street: Venture into the lively South Xizang Road Food Street, a popular spot for sampling a variety of street food favorites, from pan-fried buns to spicy noodles.

Yangpu District Food Street: Embark on a culinary adventure through Yangpu District Food Street, a vibrant neighborhood market showcasing the diverse flavors of Shanghai's street food scene.

Tips:
- Embrace the Local Experience: Venture beyond tourist hotspots and explore local neighborhoods to discover hidden street food gems frequented by locals.
- Navigate with Confidence: Be prepared to communicate in basic Mandarin or use translation apps to navigate menus and interact with vendors.
- Embrace the Adventure: Approach street food with an open mind and a sense of adventure, ready to experience new flavors and culinary delights.
- Mind Your Manners: Be mindful of local dining etiquette, such as using chopsticks correctly and disposing of food waste responsibly.
- Savor the Experience: Take your time to savor the flavors and aromas of each dish,

appreciating the culinary traditions that make Shanghai's street food scene so unique.

Upscale Dining in Shanghai

Beyond the bustling streets and vibrant street food scene, Shanghai offers a refined realm of upscale dining, where culinary artistry meets refined ambiance, creating an unforgettable gastronomic experience. From Michelin-starred establishments to elegant rooftop terraces, these culinary havens showcase the city's cosmopolitan flair and sophisticated palate.

Signature Dishes:
Braised Abalone: Indulge in the luxurious flavors of Braised Abalone, a delicate dish prepared with fresh abalone, rich sauces, and intricate garnishes.

Bird's Nest Soup: Experience the exquisite delicacy of Bird's Nest Soup, a nourishing and restorative dish believed to promote longevity and well-being.

Pan-Seared Foie Gras: Savor the rich and buttery flavors of Pan-Seared Foie Gras, a culinary masterpiece often paired with sweet accompaniments and delicate sauces.

Wagyu Beef: Experience the melt-in-your-mouth tenderness of Wagyu Beef, a premium Japanese delicacy prepared with precision and presented with artistic flair.

Poached Lobster: Indulge in the succulent flavors of Poached Lobster, a dish showcasing the freshness of the seafood and the chef's mastery of poaching techniques.

Must-Visit Upscale Dining Establishments:

Ultraviolet: Immerse yourself in the multi-sensory dining experience at Ultraviolet, a Michelin-starred restaurant that blends cutting-edge technology with culinary artistry.

8 1/2 Otto e Mezzo Bombana: Experience the refined elegance of 8 1/2 Otto e Mezzo Bombana, an Italian fine-dining establishment renowned for its impeccable service and exquisite cuisine.

Whampoa Restaurant: Discover the culinary heritage of Whampoa Restaurant, a legendary establishment offering authentic Cantonese cuisine in a refined ambiance.

M on the Bund: Indulge in the captivating views of the Bund and the Huangpu River while savoring

French cuisine at M on the Bund, a rooftop restaurant with a Michelin star.

Lost Heaven: Experience the contemporary Chinese cuisine at Lost Heaven, a stylish dining destination that blends traditional flavors with modern culinary techniques.

Tips:
- Advance Reservations: Make reservations well in advance, especially for Michelin-starred establishments and popular rooftop venues.
- Dress Code: Respect the refined ambiance of upscale dining establishments by adhering to their dress code, often requiring smart casual or formal attire.
- Mindful Dining: Approach upscale dining with a sense of appreciation and respect for the culinary artistry and the refined ambiance.
- Savor the Experience: Take your time to savor each dish, appreciating the flavors, textures, and presentation that make upscale dining an unforgettable experience.

Nightlife in Shanghai

As the sun sets over Shanghai, the city transforms into a vibrant tapestry of lights, music, and pulsating energy. From bustling nightclubs to rooftop bars with panoramic views, Shanghai's nightlife scene offers an unforgettable experience, catering to diverse tastes and preferences.

Signature Nightlife Experiences:
Immerse Yourself in the Rhythm: Dance the night away at Shanghai's lively nightclubs, where DJs spin tunes that range from electronic dance music to hip-hop and international beats.

Unwind with a Cocktail: Enjoy handcrafted cocktails and sophisticated ambiance at rooftop bars, offering breathtaking views of the city skyline and the Huangpu River.

Savor Jazz Melodies: Immerse yourself in the soulful sounds of jazz at authentic jazz clubs, where talented musicians perform in an intimate setting.

Experience Karaoke Culture: Unleash your inner pop star at Shanghai's karaoke bars, where private rooms and enthusiastic crowds create a lively and entertaining atmosphere.

Explore Hidden Gems: Venture beyond tourist hotspots and discover hidden speakeasies and underground bars, offering a unique and authentic taste of Shanghai's nightlife.

Must-Visit Nightlife Districts:
The Bund: Stroll along the iconic Bund and discover a variety of bars, restaurants, and entertainment venues, offering a captivating blend of history and modern nightlife.

Xintiandi: Immerse yourself in the vibrant atmosphere of Xintiandi, a pedestrian-friendly district lined with stylish bars, upscale restaurants, and live music venues.

M50 Creative Park: Explore the artsy enclave of M50 Creative Park, where art galleries, trendy bars, and rooftop terraces offer a unique blend of creativity and nightlife.

French Concession: Discover the charming cobblestone streets and hidden gems of the French Concession, where a mix of traditional bars, eclectic pubs, and upscale cocktail lounges await.

Jing'an District: Experience the refined and sophisticated nightlife of Jing'an District, home to luxury hotels, Michelin-starred restaurants, and elegant rooftop bars.

Tips:

- Embrace the Local Experience: Venture beyond tourist hotspots and explore local neighborhoods to discover hidden nightlife gems frequented by Shanghainese residents.
- Dress to Impress: While dress codes vary, it's generally a good idea to dress up slightly for upscale clubs and rooftop bars.
- Learn a Few Mandarin Phrases: Basic Mandarin phrases can be helpful for navigating menus, communicating with bartenders, and interacting with locals.
- Pace Yourself: Shanghai's nightlife scene is vast and diverse, so pace yourself and enjoy the experience without overindulging.
- Respect Local Customs: Be mindful of local customs and etiquette, such as avoiding loud conversations and maintaining a respectful demeanor.

Chapter 5: Shopping in Shanghai

Dive into Shanghai's captivating shopping scene, where high-end malls, bustling markets, and hidden gems await your discovery. Explore the city's top shopping destinations, from the renowned Nanjing Road to the charming Tianzifang district. Uncover a vast array of treasures, from luxury brands and designer fashions to unique handicrafts and authentic souvenirs. Embrace your inner bargain hunter with expert tips on navigating local markets and securing the best deals.

The Best Places to Shop in Shanghai

Shanghai, a bustling metropolis brimming with energy and innovation, is also a haven for shopping enthusiasts. From high-end malls to traditional markets and hidden boutiques, the city offers a diverse array of shopping experiences to suit every taste and budget.

Nanjing Road: The heart of Shanghai's shopping scene, Nanjing Road is a pedestrian-friendly paradise lined with upscale department stores, international brands, and trendy boutiques. Admire the dazzling lights and vibrant atmosphere as you browse through a vast selection of fashion, electronics, cosmetics, and souvenirs.

Tianzifang: Escape the hustle and bustle of Nanjing Road and immerse yourself in the charming ambiance of Tianzifang, a maze of narrow lanes lined with traditional Shikumen houses transformed into art galleries, cafes, and unique shops. Discover locally crafted handicrafts, vintage treasures, and one-of-a-kind souvenirs.

Shanghai Xintiandi: Experience the fusion of old and new at Shanghai Xintiandi, a pedestrian-friendly district blending traditional Shikumen architecture with modern shopping and entertainment facilities. Stroll along cobblestone streets lined with upscale boutiques, art galleries, and trendy restaurants.

Dongtai Road Antique Market: Step back in time at Dongtai Road Antique Market, a treasure trove of antiques, collectibles, and vintage finds. Haggle with vendors as you browse through a vast array of items, from jade carvings and porcelain wares to calligraphy scrolls and furniture.

Hongqiao Pearl Market: Immerse yourself in the world of pearls at Hongqiao Pearl Market, a renowned destination for pearl jewelry enthusiasts. Explore a wide range of pearls in various colors, shapes, and sizes, and witness the intricate craftsmanship of pearl stringing and jewelry making.

What to Buy in Shanghai

Shanghai, a vibrant metropolis brimming with cultural heritage and modern innovations, offers a diverse array of unique and desirable items to purchase. Whether you're seeking traditional handicrafts, authentic souvenirs, or luxury brands, Shanghai's shopping scene has something for everyone.

Traditional Handicrafts:
Silk: Renowned for its exquisite quality and timeless elegance, Shanghai silk is a must-buy for any shopper. From delicate scarves and handkerchiefs to ornate garments and home décor items, Shanghai silk embodies the city's rich textile tradition.

Jade: Prized for its beauty and symbolic significance, jade artifacts are a popular choice among collectors and those seeking a piece of Chinese heritage. Explore a variety of jade carvings, jewelry, and decorative items, each piece showcasing the craftsmanship and artistry of Chinese jade artisans.

Tea: Immerse yourself in the world of Chinese tea culture by purchasing a selection of high-quality teas from Shanghai's tea shops. From delicate green teas to robust black teas and aromatic herbal infusions, discover the nuances of Chinese tea and bring home a taste of tradition.

Calligraphy and Paintings: Appreciate the artistry of Chinese calligraphy and traditional ink paintings by purchasing these unique works of art. From elegant calligraphy scrolls to intricate landscape paintings, these pieces add a touch of sophistication to any home décor.

Authentic Souvenirs:
Shanghai Tang: Indulge in the luxurious world of Shanghai Tang, a renowned fashion house that blends traditional Chinese aesthetics with modern elegance. Purchase silk garments, handbags, accessories, and home décor items that capture the essence of Shanghai's refined style.

Shanghai No. 1 Department Store: Step into the historic Shanghai No. 1 Department Store, a beloved landmark dating back to the 1930s. Discover a wide range of locally produced goods, from traditional handicrafts and souvenirs to everyday essentials, all infused with Shanghai's unique charm.

Tianzifang Collectibles: Explore the hidden gems of Tianzifang, a charming district filled with art galleries, antique shops, and unique boutiques. Discover one-of-a-kind souvenirs, from locally crafted handicrafts and vintage treasures to quirky accessories and authentic souvenirs.

Shanghai Tea Culture Museum: Immerse yourself in the rich history of Chinese tea culture at the Shanghai Tea Culture Museum. Purchase a selection of premium teas from the museum's tea shop and learn the art of tea preparation, bringing home a piece of Shanghai's cultural heritage.

Luxury Brands:
Nanjing Road: Indulge in the world of luxury shopping along Nanjing Road, where flagship stores of renowned international brands await. From exquisite jewelry and timepieces to designer fashion and high-end electronics, Nanjing Road offers an unparalleled shopping experience.

Shanghai Xintiandi: Explore the upscale boutiques and luxury brands at Shanghai Xintiandi, a vibrant district that blends traditional Shikumen architecture with modern shopping and entertainment facilities. Discover a curated selection of fashion, accessories, and home décor from renowned designers.

Plaza 66: Experience the epitome of luxury shopping at Plaza 66, a high-end shopping mall that houses a collection of international luxury brands, including Chanel, Louis Vuitton, and Gucci. Immerse yourself in the world of opulence and indulge in the finest fashion, jewelry, and accessories.

K11 Musea: Discover a unique blend of art, culture, and luxury shopping at K11 Musea, a retail and entertainment complex that showcases contemporary art exhibitions alongside flagship stores of luxury brands. Enjoy a curated selection of high-end fashion, jewelry, and accessories in an inspiring and innovative setting.

Bargaining Tips for Shopping in Shanghai

Shanghai, a bustling metropolis renowned for its vibrant culture and dynamic shopping scene, is also a haven for bargain hunters. While fixed prices are prevalent in upscale malls and department stores, traditional markets and street vendors offer opportunities to flex your bargaining skills and secure the best deals.

Embrace the Mindset of Negotiation:
Bargaining is an integral part of the shopping experience in Shanghai's markets. Approach the process with a mindset of negotiation, understanding that it's a cultural practice and a way to establish a rapport with the vendor.

Research and Set a Target Price:
Before entering a negotiation, research the market value of the item you're interested in. This will help you set a reasonable target price and avoid overpaying.

Start Low and Negotiate Incrementally:
Begin by offering a price significantly lower than the asking price. This sets the foundation for negotiation. Be prepared to negotiate incrementally, gradually increasing your offer until you reach a mutually agreeable price.

Maintain a Friendly and Polite Demeanor:
Bargaining should be a pleasant and respectful experience. Maintain a friendly and polite demeanor throughout the negotiation. Avoid being aggressive or demanding, as this may offend the vendor.

Be Patient and Don't Rush:
Bargaining is a process and takes time. Be patient and don't rush into a decision. If you're not satisfied with the final price, you can always walk away and look for better deals elsewhere.

Learn Basic Mandarin Phrases:
Learning a few basic Mandarin phrases, such as "Duō shao qián?" (How much is this?), "Tài guì le!" (It's too expensive!), and "Piān yi dian r ba?" (Can you make it a bit cheaper?), can significantly enhance your bargaining experience.

Additional Tips:
- Observe Other Shoppers: Observe how other shoppers negotiate to get a sense of the bargaining norms and the expected price range for the item you're interested in.
- Inspect the Quality: Before committing to a purchase, carefully inspect the item for any

defects or imperfections. You may use this as leverage to negotiate a lower price.
- Consider Buying Multiple Items: If you're purchasing multiple items, consider negotiating a bulk discount. This can often lead to better deals.
- Walk Away if Necessary: Don't be afraid to walk away if you're not satisfied with the final price. There are plenty of other vendors and opportunities to find similar items elsewhere.

Chapter 6: Cultural Experiences in Shanghai

Delve into the heart of Shanghai's cultural treasures, where ancient traditions meet modern interpretations. Experience the captivating world of Chinese opera, immerse yourself in the art of tea making, master the strokes of calligraphy, discover the secrets of dumpling making, and explore the city's hidden gems on foot.

Attending a Traditional Chinese Opera Performance

In the captivating realm of Chinese performing arts, traditional Chinese opera stands as a testament to the nation's rich cultural heritage. From its mesmerizing melodies and elaborate costumes to its captivating storytelling and expressive gestures, traditional Chinese opera offers a unique and immersive cultural experience.

A Fusion of Art Forms:
Traditional Chinese opera is a harmonious blend of various art forms, including music, dance, drama, and acrobatics. The performances are typically accompanied by lively instrumental ensembles,

featuring traditional instruments such as the pipa (lute), erhu (two-stringed fiddle), and gongs.

A Spectacle of Costumes and Makeup:
Traditional Chinese opera is renowned for its elaborate and colorful costumes, which often feature intricate embroidery, silk fabrics, and symbolic motifs. The makeup of the performers is equally striking, with stylized facial designs that convey the characters' personalities and emotions.

A Tapestry of Stories and Themes:
Traditional Chinese opera draws its stories from a vast repertoire of myths, legends, historical events, and social commentary. These stories often explore themes of love, loyalty, betrayal, and the human condition, resonating deeply with audiences across generations.

Attending a Traditional Chinese Opera Performance:
Experiencing a traditional Chinese opera performance is an unforgettable cultural immersion. Here are some tips for enhancing your experience:

- Choose a Performance: Shanghai offers a variety of traditional Chinese opera venues, each with its own unique atmosphere and

repertoire. Research the different theaters and performances to find one that aligns with your interests.
- Secure Tickets: Tickets can be purchased online, at the theater box office, or through authorized ticket vendors. Plan ahead to ensure you secure tickets for the desired performance.
- Dress Appropriately: While there is no strict dress code, it's recommended to dress respectfully, avoiding overly casual attire.
- Arrive Early: Arrive at the theater early to allow time to find your seats and soak in the pre-performance ambiance.
- Embrace the Experience: Open your mind to the unique conventions of traditional Chinese opera, appreciate the artistry and storytelling, and immerse yourself in the captivating world of this ancient art form.

Visiting a Teahouse

Amidst the bustling streets and vibrant energy of Shanghai, teahouses offer havens of tranquility, where the art of tea making and the pursuit of serenity intertwine. Stepping into a traditional Shanghai teahouse is akin to entering a world of refined simplicity, where the aroma of freshly brewed tea mingles with the gentle murmur of conversation, creating an atmosphere of harmony and relaxation.

A Cultural Cornerstone:
Teahouses have long held a significant role in Chinese culture, serving as social hubs for intellectual exchange, business negotiations, and leisure activities. In Shanghai, teahouses have been an integral part of the city's social fabric for centuries, evolving from humble establishments to elegant venues that embody the city's rich cultural heritage.

A Symphony of Senses:
Entering a traditional Shanghai teahouse is a sensory journey. The gentle clinking of teacups, the soft whispers of conversations, and the delicate aroma of freshly brewed tea create a symphony of sounds and smells that soothe the mind and awaken the senses.

The Art of Tea Making:
Witnessing the art of tea making is a mesmerizing spectacle. Skilled tea masters perform a series of graceful movements, carefully selecting tea leaves, measuring the perfect proportions, and pouring hot water with precise technique. Each step is imbued with

a sense of reverence and respect for the ancient tradition of tea making.

A Ritual of Savoring:
The act of enjoying tea in a Shanghai teahouse is a ritual of savoring. Each sip is a moment of mindful appreciation, allowing the delicate flavors and aromas to wash over the palate and evoke a sense of tranquility.

Etiquette and Grace:
Teahouse etiquette emphasizes respect, mindfulness, and appreciation. Bowing slightly to the tea master as a sign of gratitude, holding the teacup with both hands, and avoiding loud conversations are all gestures that contribute to the harmonious atmosphere of the teahouse.

A Sanctuary of Serenity:
In the bustling metropolis of Shanghai, teahouses offer a sanctuary of serenity, a place to escape the daily clamor and immerse oneself in the tranquility of tea culture. Whether seeking solitude or engaging in meaningful conversations, teahouses provide a space for relaxation, reflection, and cultural enrichment.

Taking a Calligraphy Class

Calligraphy, the art of forming characters using a brush dipped in ink, is a deeply revered tradition in Chinese culture, considered an essential part of a refined education. Taking a calligraphy class in Shanghai offers an immersive experience into this ancient art form, allowing participants to master the graceful strokes and discover the profound beauty of Chinese calligraphy.

A Tapestry of History and Aesthetics:
The origins of Chinese calligraphy can be traced back to the Shang dynasty (1600-1046 BCE), and its evolution over the centuries reflects the changing aesthetics and cultural influences of Chinese civilization. More than just a means of writing, calligraphy is considered an expressive art form, capable of conveying emotions, thoughts, and philosophical concepts through the interplay of brushstrokes and ink.

The Tools of the Trade:
The essential tools of calligraphy are simple yet elegant: a brush, ink, and paper. The brush, typically made from animal hair, is the primary instrument for manipulating ink and creating strokes. Ink,

traditionally produced from soot and animal glue, offers a range of tonal variations, from delicate washes to rich blacks. Paper, often made from mulberry fibers, provides a smooth surface for the ink to flow upon.

Mastering the Strokes:
Calligraphy involves mastering a series of basic strokes, each with its unique form and technique. These strokes, ranging from fine lines to bold sweeps, form the building blocks of Chinese characters. Through practice and guidance, students learn to control the brush's pressure, direction, and speed, creating a harmonious interplay of strokes that bring characters to life.

The Art of Balance and Harmony:
Calligraphy emphasizes balance and harmony, both in the individual strokes and in the overall composition of a character. Each stroke should be executed with precision and control, yet retain a sense of fluidity and grace. The placement of characters on the paper, their relative sizes, and the overall spacing contribute to the visual harmony of the calligraphy piece.

Calligraphy as a Journey of Self-Cultivation:
The practice of calligraphy is not merely about mastering brushstrokes; it is also a journey of

self-cultivation. The discipline and focus required for calligraphy foster patience, mindfulness, and a deeper understanding of Chinese culture. As students progress, they develop a sense of aesthetic appreciation and a deeper connection to the rich heritage of Chinese calligraphy.

Learning to Make Dumplings

In the realm of Chinese cuisine, dumplings reign supreme, delicate pockets of dough filled with a symphony of flavors that tantalize the taste buds. Learning to make dumplings in Shanghai is an immersive culinary adventure, a journey into the heart of this beloved dish and the art of its preparation.

A Culinary Staple:

Dumplings, known as jiaozi in Chinese, are a ubiquitous culinary staple in Shanghai, a symbol of comfort, family gatherings, and festive occasions. Their versatility knows no bounds, with a vast array of fillings, from savory pork and vegetables to sweet red bean paste and tangy shrimp.

The Art of Dough Making:
The foundation of a perfect dumpling lies in the dough, a delicate balance of flour, water, and a touch of salt. The dough-making process is a meditative ritual, requiring precise measurements, gentle kneading, and careful resting to achieve the ideal elasticity and texture.

Shaping and Sealing:
With the dough ready, the artistry of dumpling shaping begins. Using a rolling pin, the dough is transformed into thin, circular wrappers, ready to embrace their savory or sweet fillings. Skilled hands deftly fold and pleat the wrappers, forming intricate shapes that not only enhance the dumplings' visual appeal but also secure the precious fillings within.

A Symphony of Fillings:
The world of dumpling fillings is vast and diverse, each variation offering a unique culinary experience. From the juicy succulence of pork and cabbage to the delicate sweetness of shrimp and chives, the possibilities are endless. Each filling is carefully seasoned and blended, creating a harmonious balance of flavors.

The Art of Cooking:
Once filled and sealed, dumplings embark on their final culinary journey. Traditionally, dumplings are steamed, boiled, or pan-fried, each method imparting a distinct texture and flavor profile. The steaming process preserves the dumplings' delicate flavors, while boiling adds a touch of plumpness and chewiness. Pan-frying introduces a delightful crispy exterior that contrasts with the juicy, savory interior.

A Culinary Masterpiece:
The moment of truth arrives as the perfectly cooked dumplings are presented. Each bite is a revelation, a harmonious blend of textures, flavors, and aromas. The tender, slightly chewy wrappers give way to a symphony of savory or sweet fillings, each bite a testament to the culinary mastery behind their creation.

Going on a Walking Tour of the City

Shanghai, a vibrant metropolis brimming with history, culture, and modern innovation, is best explored on foot. Walking tours offer an intimate and immersive way to discover the city's hidden gems, navigate its bustling streets, and connect with its captivating spirit.

A Tapestry of Neighborhoods:
Shanghai's diverse neighborhoods each possess a unique character, offering a glimpse into the city's rich heritage and modern evolution. From the traditional Shikumen lanes of Xintiandi to the trendy boutiques and art galleries of Tianzifang, each neighborhood reveals a different facet of Shanghai's vibrant tapestry.

Landmarks and Cultural Icons:
Immerse yourself in Shanghai's iconic landmarks, from the soaring Oriental Pearl Tower to the serene Yu Garden, a UNESCO World Heritage Site. Explore The Bund, the city's historic waterfront promenade lined with colonial-era buildings, and admire the architectural grandeur of the former French Concession.

Hidden Gems and Local Haunts:
Venture beyond the tourist hotspots and uncover Shanghai's hidden gems, tucked away in narrow alleyways and bustling markets. Discover local eateries serving authentic Shanghainese cuisine, browse through antique shops filled with treasures, and immerse yourself in the vibrant atmosphere of local markets.

A Sensory Journey:
Engage all your senses as you walk through Shanghai's streets. Inhale the aroma of freshly brewed tea wafting from traditional teahouses, savor the flavors of street food vendors, and listen to the lively chatter and traditional music that fill the air.

Connecting with the City:
Walking tours provide an opportunity to connect with Shanghai's people, their traditions, and their way of life. Engage with locals, observe their daily routines, and gain a deeper understanding of the city's unique culture.

Tips for an Enriching Walking Tour:
- Choose a Reputable Tour Operator: Select a tour operator with a good reputation and experienced guides who can provide insights into the city's history, culture, and hidden gems.
- Wear Comfortable Shoes: Walking tours involve exploring various neighborhoods and navigating streets, so ensure you wear comfortable shoes suitable for walking.
- Carry a Water Bottle: Stay hydrated throughout the tour by carrying a reusable water bottle.
- Be Mindful of Local Customs: Respect local customs and etiquette, such as avoiding loud

conversations in temples and respecting personal space in crowded areas.
- Embrace the Experience: Approach the walking tour with an open mind and a willingness to embrace the city's diversity, culture, and unexpected encounters.

Chapter 7: Day Trips from Shanghai

Embark on day trips from Shanghai and discover the captivating cities of Suzhou, Hangzhou, and Nanjing, each a gem in its own right, offering a blend of history, culture, and natural beauty.

Suzhou: A city of Canals and Gardens

In the heart of China's Jiangsu Province lies Suzhou, a mesmerizing city renowned for its intricate network of canals, graceful bridges, and serene gardens. Often referred to as the "Venice of the East," Suzhou's enchanting waterways and verdant gardens have captivated visitors for centuries, offering a tranquil escape from the bustling pace of modern life.

A Glimpse into Suzhou's Past:
Suzhou's rich history dates back over 2,500 years, making it one of China's oldest cities. During the Tang Dynasty (618-907 CE), Suzhou flourished as a prosperous center of trade and cultural exchange, earning it the title of "the Paradise on Earth." Throughout its history, Suzhou has been home to renowned poets, scholars, and artists, leaving an indelible mark on the city's cultural heritage.

Gliding Through the City's Waterways:
Embrace the tranquility of a canal cruise, gently gliding along Suzhou's waterways and admiring the picturesque scenery that unfolds along the banks. The city's canals, once essential for transportation and trade, now serve as a cherished reminder of Suzhou's rich past and a haven for leisurely exploration.

A Tapestry of Serene Gardens:
Immerse yourself in the tranquil beauty of Suzhou's renowned gardens, masterpieces of landscape design that seamlessly blend nature and art. The Humble Administrator's Garden, a UNESCO World Heritage Site, stands as a testament to the city's gardening prowess, with its intricate pavilions, winding paths, and serene ponds. Let the gentle breeze carry the fragrance of flowers as you stroll through the gardens, each step revealing a new vista of harmony and tranquility.

Exploring the City's Cultural Gems:
Venture beyond the gardens and canals to discover Suzhou's vibrant cultural attractions. Immerse yourself in the city's rich literary heritage at the Hanshan Temple, where the renowned poet Zhang Ji penned his famous poem "Farewell to Suzhou." Explore the ancient city walls, remnants of Suzhou's defensive

fortifications, and admire the architectural grandeur of the Lingbi Palace, a former Taoist monastery.

A Culinary Journey:
Indulge in Suzhou's culinary delights, where fresh seafood takes center stage. Savor the delicate flavors of steamed fish, a local specialty, or sample the city's signature dish, Suzhou-style noodles, known for their thinness and delicate texture.

Hangzhou: A Picturesque City on West Lake

Nestled amidst the verdant hills and serene waters of Zhejiang Province, Hangzhou, the capital of the Eastern Zhejiang Province, is a captivating city renowned for its picturesque West Lake, a UNESCO World Heritage Site. Often referred to as the "Paradise on Earth," Hangzhou's enchanting beauty has captivated poets, artists, and travelers for centuries, inspiring odes to its serene landscapes and timeless elegance.

A Haven of Natural Beauty:
West Lake, the heart and soul of Hangzhou, is a shimmering expanse of water, adorned with willow

trees swaying gently in the breeze, graceful pagodas reflecting their silhouettes against the tranquil surface, and verdant hills framing the enchanting scenery. Stroll along the lake's serene shores, where ancient causeways and picturesque bridges connect the lake's tranquil islands, each offering a unique perspective of this mesmerizing landscape.

A Legacy of Cultural Gems:
Immerse yourself in Hangzhou's rich cultural heritage, evident in its numerous temples, pagodas, and gardens that dot the city's landscape. Ascend the Leifeng Pagoda, a symbol of Hangzhou's enduring beauty, and admire the panoramic views of West Lake from its lofty heights. Explore the serene Lingyin Temple, nestled amidst verdant hills, and witness the grandeur of the gigantic Feilai Peak, a natural rock formation that resembles a Buddha's head.

A Culinary Symphony:
Indulge in Hangzhou's culinary delights, a symphony of flavors that reflect the city's rich heritage and fresh local ingredients. Savor the delicate flavors of Longjing tea, a renowned specialty known for its subtle sweetness and refreshing aroma. Sample the city's signature dish, West Lake Vinegar-Dressed Fish, a

culinary masterpiece where tender fish is enveloped in a tangy and aromatic vinegar sauce.

Nanjing: The Former Capital of Six Dynasties

Nestled along the banks of the mighty Yangtze River, Nanjing, the capital of Jiangsu Province, is a city steeped in history and cultural grandeur. Renowned as the former capital of six dynasties, Nanjing boasts a rich tapestry of historical landmarks, ancient temples, and vibrant cultural attractions, offering a captivating glimpse into China's illustrious past.

A Glimpse into Nanjing's Past:
Nanjing's history stretches back over 2,500 years, making it one of China's oldest cities. The city served as the capital of six dynasties, each leaving an indelible mark on its architecture, culture, and traditions. From the Eastern Wu Dynasty (222-280 CE) to the Ming Dynasty (1368-1644 CE), Nanjing flourished as a center of political, economic, and cultural influence, shaping China's historical trajectory.

A Majestic City Wall:
Embark on a walk along the Nanjing City Wall, one of the world's longest city walls, stretching over 22 kilometers. Witness the grandeur of this ancient fortification, a testament to Nanjing's enduring legacy. Ascend the towers and admire the panoramic views of the city, where modern skyscrapers blend seamlessly with historical landmarks, creating a captivating contrast of the past and present.

A Symbol of Resilience:
Pay your respects at the Zhongshan Gate, a monumental archway that stands as a symbol of Nanjing's resilience. This imposing structure, originally built during the Ming Dynasty, has witnessed centuries of conflict and change, yet it remains a steadfast reminder of the city's enduring spirit.

A Sanctuary for Historical Figures:
Visit the Mausoleum of Dr. Sun Yat-sen, the revered founder of the Republic of China. Wander through the serene gardens and pay homage to this visionary leader who played a pivotal role in shaping modern China. Immerse yourself in the tranquility of the Meiling Palace, the former residence of Dr. Sun Yat-sen and his wife, Soong Ching-ling.

A Memorial to a Tragic Past:
Reflect on the somber history at the Nanjing Massacre Memorial, a poignant reminder of the devastating Nanjing Massacre of 1937. Walk through the museum's exhibits, each piece bearing witness to the atrocities of war and the resilience of the human spirit.

A Culinary Adventure:
Indulge in Nanjing's culinary delights, a symphony of flavors that reflect the city's rich heritage and fresh local ingredients. Savor the delicate flavors of Xiaolongbao, soup-filled dumplings known for their thin, delicate skins and flavorful broth. Sample the city's signature dish, Salted Duck, a savory delicacy where duck is preserved in a traditional salt-curing process.

How to Get There

Suzhou

High-Speed Train: The most convenient and comfortable way to travel from Shanghai to Suzhou is by high-speed train. High-speed trains depart from Shanghai Hongqiao Railway Station and Shanghai Station, arriving at Suzhou Station in approximately 30 minutes. Tickets can be purchased online or at the train station.

Bus: Bus travel is a more affordable option but takes longer than the high-speed train. Buses depart from Shanghai's Long-distance Bus Station and arrive at Suzhou's South Bus Station in approximately 2 hours. Tickets can be purchased online or at the bus station.

Day Trip Packages: Numerous tour operators offer day trip packages to Suzhou, providing transportation, guided tours, and meals. This is a convenient option for those who prefer a hassle-free experience.

Independent Travel: If you prefer independent travel, plan your itinerary carefully, considering transportation options, attractions, and dining options.

Hangzhou

High-Speed Train: High-speed trains are the fastest and most convenient way to travel from Shanghai to Hangzhou. Trains depart from Shanghai Hongqiao Railway Station and Shanghai Station, arriving at Hangzhou East Railway Station in approximately 45 minutes. Tickets can be purchased online or at the train station.

Bus: Bus travel is a more affordable option but takes longer than the high-speed train. Buses depart from Shanghai's Long-distance Bus Station and arrive at Hangzhou's West Lake Bus Station in approximately 2 hours. Tickets can be purchased online or at the bus station.

Day Trip Packages: Numerous tour operators offer day trip packages to Hangzhou, providing transportation, guided tours, and meals. This is a convenient option for those who prefer a hassle-free experience.

Independent Travel: If you prefer independent travel, plan your itinerary carefully, considering transportation options, attractions, and dining options.

Nanjing

High-Speed Train: High-speed trains are the fastest and most convenient way to travel from Shanghai to Nanjing. Trains depart from Shanghai Hongqiao Railway Station and Shanghai Station, arriving at Nanjing South Railway Station in approximately 1 hour and 30 minutes. Tickets can be purchased online or at the train station.

Bus: Bus travel is a more affordable option but takes longer than the high-speed train. Buses depart from Shanghai's Long-distance Bus Station and arrive at Nanjing's Jiangning Bus Station in approximately 3 hours. Tickets can be purchased online or at the bus station.

Day Trip Packages: Numerous tour operators offer day trip packages to Nanjing, providing transportation, guided tours, and meals. This is a convenient option for those who prefer a hassle-free experience.

Independent Travel: If you prefer independent travel, plan your itinerary carefully, considering transportation options, attractions, and dining options.

Chapter 8: Practical Information for Visitors

Navigate the intricacies of language and communication, understand local etiquette and customs, ensure your health and safety, and access emergency contact information for a seamless and enriching Shanghai experience.

Language and Communication

Effective communication is a cornerstone of a fulfilling travel experience, and mastering the basics of Shanghai's language and etiquette can significantly enhance your interactions with locals. While Mandarin Chinese is the official language of China, Shanghainese, a local dialect, is widely spoken in the city.

Mandarin Chinese Essentials:

Greetings and Farewells:
- 你好 (nǐ hǎo) – Hello
- 再见 (zài jiàn) – Goodbye
- Asking for Directions:

- 请问XX在哪里？(qǐng wèn XX zài nǎ lǐ?) – Excuse me, where is XX?
- 我想去XX，怎么走？(Wǒ xiǎng qù XX, zěn me zǒu?) – I want to go to XX, how do I get there?

Expressing Gratitude:
- 谢谢 (xiè xiè) – Thank you
- 不客气 (bù kè qì) – You're welcome

Shanghainese Phrases:

Greetings and Farewells:
- 侬好 (nóng hǎo) – Hello
- 再会 (zài huì) – Goodbye

Asking for Directions:
- XX勒啥地方？(XX lè shén me dì fāng?) – Where is XX?
- 额要去XX，咋个走？(É wù qù XX, zǎ ge zǒu?) – I want to go to XX, how do I get there?

Cultural Communication Tips:
- Address with Respect: Use titles like 先生 (xiān shēng) for men and 女士 (nǚ shì) for women when addressing someone for the first time.

- Business Cards: Exchanging business cards is customary in business settings. Present your card with both hands and hold the recipient's card respectfully.
- Avoid Loud Conversations: Chinese culture emphasizes politeness and respectful behavior. Avoid loud conversations in public places, such as restaurants and temples.

Language Learning Resources:
- Mobile Apps: Duolingo, Memrise, and HelloChinese offer interactive Mandarin learning experiences.
- Online Courses: iTalki, Yoyo Chinese, and ChinesePod offer structured Mandarin courses with native instructors.
- Language Exchange Platforms: Converse with native Shanghainese speakers through platforms like Tandem and HelloTalk.

Etiquette and Customs

Immersing yourself in Shanghai's vibrant culture extends beyond exploring its iconic landmarks and savoring its culinary delights. Understanding and respecting local etiquette and customs is essential for a seamless and enriching travel experience. Here's a guide to navigating the cultural landscape of Shanghai:

Greetings and Introductions:
Handshakes: Handshakes are common in business settings, with a firm, brief grip. In social situations, a slight bow with a smile is more appropriate.

Formal Introductions: Use titles like 先生 (xiān shēng) for men and 女士 (nǚ shì) for women when addressing someone for the first time.

Gift Giving: If invited to a home, bring a small gift, such as flowers or fruits. Avoid giving gifts of knives or mirrors, which are considered unlucky.

Dining Etiquette:
Chopsticks: Hold chopsticks with the thicker end between your thumb and index finger, resting the thinner end on the chopstick rest. Avoid sticking chopsticks upright in rice, a gesture associated with funerals.

Sharing Food: Sharing dishes is customary in Chinese dining culture. Use serving chopsticks to transfer food to others' plates.

Finishing Your Plate: Leaving a small amount of food on your plate indicates that you are satisfied with the meal.

Social Etiquette:
Respect Personal Space: Avoid overly physical contact, such as back-patting or hugging, as this can be considered intrusive.

Noise Levels: Maintain a moderate volume in public places, such as restaurants and temples.

Queueing: Form orderly queues when waiting in line. Respect the personal space of those in front of you.

General Tips:
Dress Code: Dress modestly, especially when visiting temples or other religious sites.

Pointing: Avoid pointing directly at people or objects. Use a hand gesture or phrase instead.

Photography: Seek permission before taking photos of people, especially in private or sensitive settings.

Cultural Sensitivity:

Language Barriers: While English is increasingly understood in Shanghai, be patient and understanding when encountering language barriers.

Cultural Differences: Respect cultural differences and avoid making assumptions or comparisons.

Openness and Curiosity: Approach cultural interactions with an open mind and a willingness to learn new customs.

Health and Safety Tips

General Health Tips
- Vaccinations: Ensure you are up-to-date on recommended vaccinations before traveling to China.
- Tap Water: Avoid drinking tap water as it may not be safe. Purchase bottled water or use a water filter.
- Food Safety: Choose reputable restaurants and avoid street food vendors that may not adhere to proper food safety standards.

- Air Quality: Shanghai's air quality can vary, so be prepared with a face mask, especially during periods of high pollution.
- Sun Protection: Apply sunscreen and wear protective clothing, especially during the summer months.

Medical Care
- Travel Insurance: Obtain travel insurance that covers medical expenses in case of illness or injury.
- Hospitals and Clinics: International hospitals and clinics are available in Shanghai, offering English-speaking medical professionals.
- Pharmacies: Pharmacies are widely available and carry a variety of medications, both over-the-counter and prescription.

Safety Precautions
- Petty Theft: Be mindful of your belongings in crowded areas and tourist attractions. Keep valuables secure and avoid carrying large amounts of cash.
- Scams: Be aware of common scams, such as fake taxi drivers or individuals offering counterfeit goods.

- Traffic Safety: Exercise caution when crossing streets, as traffic can be unpredictable. Use designated crosswalks and follow traffic signals.
- Emergency Contact Information: Save emergency contact information, including local police and medical services.
- Language Barriers: Carry a phrasebook or translation app to facilitate communication with locals in case of emergencies.

Additional Tips
- Learn Basic Phrases: Learn a few basic Mandarin Chinese phrases, such as "help" (救命) and "I need a doctor" (我需要医生), for emergencies.
- Register with Your Embassy: Register your travel details with your embassy or consulate for assistance in case of emergencies.
- Stay Informed: Stay updated on local news and weather conditions, especially during typhoon season.
- Trust Your Instincts: If a situation feels unsafe, trust your instincts and avoid it.
- Enjoy the Experience: Relax, be mindful of your surroundings, and enjoy your time exploring the vibrant city of Shanghai.

Emergency Contact Information

Here is a list of emergency contact information for visitors to Shanghai:

Police
- Shanghai Emergency Hotline: 110

Fire
- Shanghai Fire Department: 119

Medical Emergencies
- Shanghai Emergency Medical Center: 120
- Shanghai International Medical Center: 021-6384-4444
- Shanghai General Hospital: 021-2320-9999

Traffic Accidents
- Shanghai Traffic Accident Emergency Hotline: 122

Travel Assistance
- U.S. Consulate General Shanghai: +86 21 6188 5000
- British Consulate-General Shanghai: +86 21 6108 1666

- Canadian Consulate General Shanghai: +86 21 6311 3959
- Australian Consulate-General Shanghai: +86 21 6139 7400
- Shanghai Tourism Information Center: +86 21 6328 1000
- Shanghai Foreigners Service Center: +86 21 6352 4513
- Emergency Translation Service: 962288

Chapter 9: Travel Cost

Delve into the financial aspects of your Shanghai adventure, exploring average daily expenses for budget-conscious, mid-range, and luxury travelers. Understand the factors that can influence your costs and discover practical tips for savoring Shanghai without breaking the bank.

Average Daily Expenses for Budget, Mid-range, and Luxury travelers

Here is a breakdown of average daily expenses for budget, mid-range, and luxury travelers in Shanghai:

Budget Travelers (Average Daily Expenses: ¥100-200)

Accommodation:
- Hostels: ¥50-100 per night
- Budget guesthouses: ¥100-150 per night

Food:
- Street food: ¥20-30 per meal
- Budget restaurants: ¥30-50 per meal

Transportation:
- Public buses: ¥2-5 per trip
- Metro: ¥3-10 per trip

Activities:
- Free walking tours
- Visiting parks and temples
- Exploring local markets

Mid-range Travelers (Average Daily Expenses: ¥200-500)

Accommodation:
- Mid-range hotels: ¥200-300 per night
- Serviced apartments: ¥300-400 per night

Food:
- Casual restaurants: ¥50-80 per meal
- Mid-range local eateries: ¥80-120 per meal

Transportation:
- Taxis: ¥20-30 for short trips
- Bike rental: ¥20-50 per day

Activities:
- Paid walking tours

- Visiting museums and attractions
- Experiencing local nightlife

Luxury Travelers (Average Daily Expenses: ¥500+)

Accommodation:
- Luxury hotels: ¥500+ per night
- Luxury serviced apartments: ¥1,000+ per night

Food:
- Fine dining restaurants: ¥200+ per meal
- Michelin-starred restaurants: ¥500+ per meal

Transportation:
- Private car services: ¥200-300 per day
- Limousine services: ¥500+ per day

Activities:
- Exclusive tours and experiences
- Attend theater performances or concerts
- Shopping at high-end boutiques

Factors that Can Affect Your Travel Costs

Accommodation

Accommodation Type: The type of accommodation you choose will significantly impact your overall travel costs. Hostels and budget guesthouses offer the most affordable options, while luxury hotels and serviced apartments cater to those seeking a more opulent experience.

Location: Accommodation costs vary depending on the location. Staying in central areas, such as The Bund or the French Concession, will be more expensive than in less popular neighborhoods. Consider staying slightly further out from the city center to save on accommodation costs.

Booking in Advance: Booking your accommodation in advance, especially during peak seasons, can help secure better rates and avoid last-minute price surges.

Food

Dining Options: Shanghai offers a diverse range of dining options, from street food stalls and local eateries to fine dining restaurants and Michelin-starred establishments. Your food expenses will depend on the type of cuisine and dining experience you prefer.

Street Food and Local Eateries: Indulge in Shanghai's vibrant street food scene and explore local restaurants to experience authentic flavors at affordable prices.

Fine Dining: If you're seeking a more refined culinary experience, be prepared for higher prices at upscale restaurants and Michelin-starred establishments.

Transportation
Transportation Modes: Shanghai's efficient public transportation system, including buses, metro, and taxis, offers convenient and cost-effective ways to travel around the city.

Distance and Frequency: Transportation costs will depend on the distance you travel and the frequency of your trips. Consider purchasing a Shanghai Public Transportation Card for discounted fares.

Private Car Services: For added convenience and flexibility, consider using private car services or limousine services, but be prepared for higher costs.

Activities

Free Activities: Take advantage of Shanghai's numerous free attractions, such as parks, temples, and cultural centers, to save on your sightseeing expenses.

Paid Activities: Explore Shanghai's diverse range of paid activities, including museums, historical sites, theme parks, and cultural performances. Prioritize activities that align with your interests and budget.

Exclusive Experiences: For a more personalized and immersive experience, consider indulging in exclusive tours, private guides, and special events, but be prepared for premium pricing.

Additional Factors

Seasonality: Travel during peak seasons, such as Chinese New Year and Golden Week, can lead to higher accommodation, transportation, and attraction prices. Consider traveling during off-seasons to save on costs.

Shopping: Shanghai's diverse shopping scene caters to all budgets. From bustling local markets to high-end boutiques and luxury brands, your shopping expenses will depend on your preferences and budget.

Entertainment: Shanghai offers a vibrant nightlife scene, with bars, clubs, and live music venues. Your entertainment expenses will depend on your preferences and the type of venues you visit.

Chapter 10: Further Exploration

Augment your Shanghai experience with essential planning resources, explore curated itineraries tailored to your style, and venture beyond the city limits to discover neighboring gems.

Additional Resources for Planning Your Trip to Shanghai

Here are some additional resources for planning your trip to Shanghai:

Official Tourism Websites:
- Shanghai Municipal Tourism Administration: https://m.shanghaitour.net/live/all/
- Shanghai Tourism Information Center: https://www.meet-in-shanghai.net/

Travel Blogs and Websites:
The Culture Trip:
- https://theculturetrip.com/asia/china/shanghai

Expert Vagabond:
- https://expertvagabond.com/

Travel Caffeine:
- https://www.travelcaffeine.com/shanghai-china-trip-planning-guide/

Transportation Resources:

Shanghai Metro:
- https://www.travelchinaguide.com/cityguides/shanghai/transportation/metro-subway-map.htm

Shanghai Buses:
- https://www.sptcc.com/

Shanghai Taxis:
- https://www.shanghai-taxi.com/

Accommodation Resources:

Hostelworld:
- https://www.hostelworld.com/

Airbnb:
- https://www.airbnb.com/

Hotels.com:
- https://www.hotels.com/

Language Learning Resources:
Duolingo:
- https://www.duolingo.com/

Memrise:
- https://www.memrise.com/

HelloChinese:
- https://www.youtube.com/watch?v=g5dxoc7zEBE

Culture and Etiquette Guides:
China Intercultural Communication Center:
- https://en.cicc.com/

Confucius Institute:
- https://ci.cn/en/

Cultural Atlas of China:
- https://culturalatlas.sbs.com.au/chinese-culture

Suggested Itineraries for Different Types of Travelers

History and Culture Enthusiast

Day 1:
Morning: Explore the Yu Garden, a serene oasis amidst Shanghai's bustling streets. Admire the intricate architecture, stroll through tranquil gardens, and experience traditional tea culture.

Afternoon: Immerse yourself in Shanghai's rich history at the Shanghai Museum, a treasure trove of Chinese artifacts and art spanning over 5,000 years.

Evening: Wander through the atmospheric lanes of Tianzifang, a charming former French Concession district now filled with art galleries, boutiques, and local eateries.

Day 2:
Morning: Visit the Bund, Shanghai's iconic waterfront promenade, and admire the contrasting architecture of the old and new city.

Afternoon: Delve into Shanghai's revolutionary past at the Xin Tian Di, a complex of restored historic buildings and museums commemorating the Chinese Revolution.

Evening: Indulge in a traditional Shanghai opera performance at the Shanghai Grand Theater, a cultural landmark showcasing the city's artistic heritage.

Foodie and Culinary Adventurer

Day 1:
Morning: Embark on a culinary adventure through Nanxiang Mantoudian, the birthplace of the iconic Xiaolongbao, delicate soup dumplings.

Afternoon: Explore the bustling streets of Wukang Road, lined with trendy cafes, traditional teahouses, and authentic Shanghainese restaurants.

Evening: Savor a delectable dinner at a Michelin-starred restaurant, such as Yongfu or Da Dong, and indulge in the city's refined culinary scene.

Day 2:
Morning: Visit the Shanghai Farmers' Market, a vibrant hub of local produce and traditional Chinese delicacies.

Sample fresh fruits, savor street food snacks, and immerse yourself in the lively market atmosphere.

Afternoon: Take a cooking class and learn to prepare authentic Shanghainese dishes, such as red braised pork belly or stir-fried noodles with shrimp.

Evening: Conclude your culinary journey with a traditional Shanghainese hotpot dinner, a communal dining experience filled with flavors and aromas.

Family-Friendly Adventure

Day 1:
Morning: Unleash your inner child at Shanghai Disneyland, a magical realm of Disney characters, exhilarating rides, and enchanting shows.

Afternoon: Discover the wonders of the underwater world at Shanghai Ocean Aquarium, home to diverse marine life from around the globe.

Evening: Take a relaxing cruise along the Huangpu River, admiring the city's illuminated skyline and enjoying live entertainment.

Day 2:
Morning: Visit the Shanghai Natural History Museum, a fascinating exploration of the planet's natural wonders, from dinosaurs to ecosystems.

Afternoon: Explore the Shanghai Children's Museum, a vibrant and interactive space designed to engage and educate young minds with hands-on exhibits.

Evening: Enjoy a family-friendly performance at the Shanghai Circus World, a mesmerizing spectacle of acrobatics, stunts, and colorful costumes.

Tips for Planning Your Itinerary

Consider the duration of your trip: Having a clear understanding of how long you'll be in Shanghai will help you plan your itinerary effectively. Decide on the number of days you'll be spending in the city and allocate time accordingly for different activities and attractions.

Identify your interests and priorities: What are you most excited about experiencing in Shanghai? Are you a history buff, a culinary enthusiast, or a nature lover?

Prioritize the activities and attractions that align with your interests and preferences.

Research and gather information: Familiarize yourself with Shanghai's must-see attractions, hidden gems, and local experiences. Read reviews, check travel blogs, and explore online resources to get a comprehensive understanding of what the city has to offer.

Consider your travel style: Are you a spontaneous traveler or do you prefer a more structured plan? If you enjoy flexibility, leave some room in your itinerary for spontaneous discoveries. If you prefer a more organized approach, create a detailed schedule with planned activities and transportation arrangements.

Balance popular attractions with off-the-beaten-path experiences: While visiting iconic landmarks is essential, don't overlook the unique experiences found in lesser-known neighborhoods and local markets. Immerse yourself in the authentic side of Shanghai by venturing off the beaten path.

Factor in transportation and logistics: Plan your transportation between attractions and accommodations to avoid unnecessary time spent commuting. Consider using public transportation, taxis, or ride-hailing services depending on your preferences and budget.

Allow time for unexpected delays: Unexpected events or delays can happen, so be sure to incorporate some buffer time into your itinerary. This will help you avoid feeling rushed and allow you to enjoy each activity without stress.

Be flexible and adaptable: Things don't always go according to plan when traveling, so be prepared to adjust your itinerary as needed. Embrace spontaneity and enjoy the unexpected twists and turns that make travel so enriching.

Conclusion

Shanghai, a city that pulsates with energy, exudes history, and tantalizes the senses, has undoubtedly left an indelible mark on your travel journey. From its towering skyscrapers to its hidden alleyways, from its bustling markets to its tranquil temples, Shanghai has unveiled its many facets, inviting you to delve into its vibrant tapestry. As you bid farewell to this captivating metropolis, let the memories of your Shanghai adventure linger on.

Carry with you the echoes of laughter shared with newfound friends, the taste of culinary delights that danced on your palate, and the kaleidoscope of colors that painted your vision. Remember the warmth of encounters with locals, the awe-inspiring moments amidst architectural grandeur, and the tranquility found in moments of solitude.

Shanghai has whispered its secrets to you, revealing its rich heritage, its dynamic spirit, and its unwavering resilience. As you depart, let the city's spirit continue to inspire you, reminding you to embrace the unexpected, celebrate diversity, and savor the beauty that lies within every corner of the world.

Picture on the cover was downloaded from freepik

<a href="https://www.freepik.com/free-photo/shanghai-sunset_29452332.htm#query=SHANGHAI&position=28&from_view=search&track=sph&uuid=59165597-c215-4608-9b91-5bca18e99298">Image by TravelScape</a> on Freepik